Artificial Intelligence and Machine Learning in Cybersecurity

Artificial Intelligence and Machine Learning in Cybersecurity: A Comprehensive Guide to Improving Cybersecurity Protocol is a comprehensive exploration of the intersection between cutting-edge technology and cybersecurity practices. This book offers readers an in-depth understanding of how artificial intelligence (AI) and machine learning (ML) are reshaping the cybersecurity landscape. It begins with foundational concepts, explaining AI and ML's principles and their transformative potential within various sectors, particularly cybersecurity. This book uniquely combines theoretical insights and practical applications, making it an essential resource for graduate students and cybersecurity professionals eager to expand their knowledge and skills.

The book's uniqueness lies in its detailed analysis of how AI and ML can predict and counteract emerging threats in real time, shifting the paradigm from reactive to proactive cybersecurity measures. By delving into a wide range of topics, such as AI-powered Intrusion Detection and Prevention Systems (IDPS) and endpoint security, the author provides case studies and examples from sectors like finance and healthcare. This hands-on approach not only illustrates successful implementations but also highlights potential challenges, offering balanced perspectives and strategies to overcome hurdles. The inclusion of ethical considerations around AI usage in cybersecurity further distinguishes it as a forward-thinking guide.

As cyber threats continue to evolve, the need for advanced AI and ML methodologies becomes increasingly critical. This book addresses this urgency by equipping readers with contemporary knowledge and tools necessary to leverage these technologies effectively. The discussion of future trends, such as AI-powered quantum security and necessary policy implications, ensures that readers are well-prepared to navigate the complexities of cybersecurity in the coming decades. Ultimately, it serves as both an educational textbook for students and a practical guide for cyber practitioners, offering a roadmap for implementing AI-driven cybersecurity solutions that enhance threat detection, response, and prevention.

Artificial Intelligence and Machine Learning in Cybersecurity

A Comprehensive Guide to Improving Cybersecurity Protocol

Richard Gwashy Young, PhD

Routledge
Taylor & Francis Group

A PRODUCTIVITY PRESS BOOK

Designed cover image: Web Large Image (Public)

First published 2025
by Routledge
605 Third Avenue, New York, NY 10158

and by Routledge
4 Park Square, Milton Park, Abingdon, Oxon, OX14 4RN

Routledge is an imprint of the Taylor & Francis Group, an informa business

© 2025 Richard Young, Ph.D

ISBN: 978-1-041-01486-7 (hbk)
ISBN: 978-1-041-01485-0 (pbk)
ISBN: 978-1-003-61502-6 (ebk)

DOI: 10.4324/9781003615026

Typeset in ITC Garamond Std
by Deanta Global Publishing Services, Chennai, India

Dedication

To all the cybersecurity professionals dedicated to safeguarding our digital world, your unwavering commitment and relentless pursuit of knowledge inspire us all. This book is dedicated to those who work tirelessly behind the scenes, often facing unseen threats with resilience and innovation. May this work serve as a beacon, empowering you to harness the transformative power of artificial intelligence and machine learning in the ever-evolving landscape of cybersecurity. Together, we strive for a safer future.

Contents

Preface

In today's digital landscape, the stakes have never been higher. As organizations increasingly rely on technology to drive operations, the cybersecurity threats facing them continue to evolve at an alarming pace. Traditional methods of defense are no longer sufficient to combat the sophisticated tactics employed by cybercriminals. In this context, the integration of artificial intelligence (AI) and machine learning (ML) into cybersecurity protocols is not just an option; it is a necessity.

This book, *Artificial Intelligence and Machine Learning in Cybersecurity: A Comprehensive Guide to Improving Cybersecurity Protocol*, aims to illuminate the transformative potential of AI and ML in enhancing our defenses against cyber threats. Drawing from almost three decades of experience in the information and cybersecurity domain, I have witnessed firsthand the rapid advancements in technology and their implications for security strategies. I have also observed the challenges that organizations face in navigating this landscape. My goal is to provide a comprehensive guide that demystifies AI and ML while offering practical insights on their application within cybersecurity frameworks.

Throughout this journey, we will explore the foundational concepts of AI and ML, the current state of the cybersecurity landscape, and the ways in which these technologies can revolutionize our approach to threat detection, response, and prevention. Each chapter is designed to equip cybersecurity practitioners, decision-makers, and students with the knowledge and tools necessary to implement innovative security solutions in their environments.

As we delve into the intersection of AI, Machine Learning, and cybersecurity, I invite you to consider the broader implications of these technologies, including ethical considerations, policy implications, and the continuous need for adaptation and learning. The future of cybersecurity is not solely dependent on technology; it is also shaped by the people who design, implement, and manage these systems.

I hope this book serves as a valuable resource and inspiration for all those dedicated to improving cybersecurity protocols and fostering a safer digital environment for individuals and organizations alike. Together, let us embrace the opportunities presented by AI and ML, ensuring that we not only protect our systems but also pave the way for a more resilient and secure future.

Acknowledgments

To my mentors and colleagues, whose wisdom and collaboration have enriched my journey in this field. Your guidance has shaped my understanding of the complexities of cybersecurity and the transformative potential of artificial intelligence and machine learning.

Lastly, to my family, whose support and encouragement have been my anchor throughout this endeavor. Your belief in my vision fuels my passion for advancing our collective knowledge and practices in cybersecurity. Thank you for being my greatest motivation.

About the Author

Richard Young is a seasoned cybersecurity leader and practitioner with over 30 years of experience in the financial services industry. Serving as an adjunct professor and Cybersecurity Program chair, he has made significant contributions to academia, leading the development of innovative curricula that bridge the gap between theoretical knowledge and practical application. His teaching expertise includes cybersecurity, IT risk, and leadership, where he has mentored numerous graduate students and future leaders in navigating complex cybersecurity challenges. Currently, Dr. Young serves as the head of Global Operations Tech Risk & Platforms Engineering at Citibank in New York City where he spearheads technical product ownership and risk management strategies across regions. His previous roles as chief information security officer at Barclays and Deutsche Bank have equipped him with extensive expertise in establishing and maintaining enterprise strategies to protect information assets. Dr. Young is recognized for delivering operational excellence, implementing regulatory reforms, and fostering collaborative relationships across global financial institutions.

In addition to his extensive professional experience, Dr. Young holds a PhD in Leadership with a focus on the Management of Information Systems and is pursuing an EdD in Educational Leadership. He is the author of three influential books, including *The 2nd Coming: The Recolonization of Africa by the East, Cybersecurity – A Handbook for Boards and C-Suite, and Leadership Practices for Optimizing Performance and Job Satisfaction in the Financial Industry*. Dr. Young's insights and thought leadership have made him a prominent figure in bridging technology and cybersecurity, preparing organizations for the future challenges of the digital landscape.

Introduction

The digital world is a double-edged sword; while it offers unprecedented opportunities for innovation, collaboration, and growth, it also presents a myriad of vulnerabilities that cyber adversaries eagerly exploit. As organizations increasingly depend on interconnected systems to operate efficiently, the potential impact of a cybersecurity breach has escalated dramatically. From devastating financial losses to irreparable damage to reputation, the consequences of inadequate cybersecurity measures are more pronounced today than ever before.

In response to this evolving threat landscape, the adoption of artificial intelligence (AI) and machine learning (ML) has emerged as a beacon of hope in the cybersecurity arena. These technologies offer the ability to analyze vast amounts of data, detect anomalies, and respond to threats with remarkable speed and accuracy. Yet, despite their potential, the effective integration of AI and ML into cybersecurity frameworks remains a daunting challenge for many organizations. This book aims to address that gap by providing a comprehensive exploration of how these technologies can significantly enhance cybersecurity protocols.

The journey begins by establishing a foundational understanding of AI and ML, outlining their evolution, core concepts, and relevance to cybersecurity. We will then delve into the pressing challenges that organizations face in securing their digital assets, examining emerging threats such as advanced persistent threats (APTs), ransomware, and insider threats. This exploration serves as a backdrop for illustrating how AI and ML can not only improve threat detection and response but also redefine the landscape of proactive cybersecurity measures.

Throughout this book, you will find practical insights, real-world case studies, and strategic recommendations designed for cybersecurity practitioners, decision-makers, and students alike. Each chapter is crafted to empower you with the knowledge necessary to leverage AI and ML effectively, ensuring that your organization can stay one step ahead of cybercriminals.

Furthermore, as we navigate the complexities of implementing AI-driven security solutions, we must also consider the ethical implications and challenges that arise. Questions of bias in algorithms, privacy considerations, and the potential for misuse of AI technologies will be explored, highlighting the importance of responsible implementation in fostering trust and security.

In closing this introduction, I encourage you to engage with the material actively and consider how the principles discussed can be applied in your unique context. The world of cybersecurity is not static; it is a dynamic field that requires continuous learning and adaptation. As we embark on this journey together, let us embrace the transformative potential of AI and ML, setting the stage for a future where our defenses are as advanced as the threats we seek to thwart.

Welcome to the exploration of leveraging artificial intelligence and machine learning to improve cybersecurity protocols. Together, we can shape a safer digital landscape for all.

Chapter 1

Introduction to AI, ML, and Cybersecurity

1.1 Overview of AI and ML: Definitions, Evolution, and Applications in Various Industries

In this introductory chapter, we delve into the transformative impact of Artificial Intelligence (AI) and Machine Learning (ML) on cybersecurity protocols. As these technologies continue to advance, they offer both unprecedented opportunities and formidable challenges. By understanding the evolution, potential applications, and risks associated with AI and ML, cybersecurity professionals can better prepare to harness these tools for enhancing organizational defenses while remaining vigilant against their misuse.

In recent years, the convergence of artificial intelligence (AI) and machine learning (ML) with cybersecurity has fundamentally altered the landscape of digital defense. As organizations across various industries grapple with an increasingly complex and hostile cyber threat environment, understanding these advanced technologies is crucial not only for threat mitigation but also for protecting sensitive information in a rapidly evolving digital economy. This introduction sets the stage for our exploration of AI and ML's foundational roles in cybersecurity, detailing their evolution, applications, and the dual-edged nature of their use in both malicious and defensive capacities.

1.1.1 The Evolution of AI and ML in the Context of Cybersecurity and Threat Intelligence

The journey of AI and ML began in the mid-20th century, with the aim of simulating human intelligence through algorithms and computational models. Initial efforts were rudimentary, focusing primarily on rule-based systems. However, as computing power increased and data generation exploded in the 21st century, the potential of AI and ML catapulted to prominence.

In the context of cybersecurity, the relevance of AI and ML became evident as organizations faced unprecedented cyber threats that traditional security measures struggled to address. The exponential growth in data, coupled with increasingly sophisticated attacks, necessitated innovative solutions. As businesses began leveraging AI and ML technologies, cybersecurity practices evolved from reactive strategies to proactive and predictive ones. This evolution heralded the use of sophisticated algorithms capable of identifying anomalies, predicting potential breaches, and automating threat responses. Consequently, AI and ML have redefined threat intelligence, enabling organizations to enhance their risk management protocols and build resilient cybersecurity infrastructures.

1.1.1.1 Threat Actors' Use of AI and ML to Breach Organizational Systems

While AI and ML hold promise for improving organizational security, these technologies are equally appealing to threat actors looking to exploit vulnerabilities. Cybercriminals can employ AI-driven algorithms to enhance their attack methodologies, thereby increasing their effectiveness and stealth.

For instance, sophisticated bots can execute automated phishing attacks by analyzing large data sets to craft convincing emails tailored to evade traditional filters (Figure 1.1). Additionally, ML algorithms can analyze network traffic patterns, allowing attackers to identify weak points for breaching systems. Ransomware has also experienced a metamorphosis due to AI; criminals can employ ML to optimize their payloads, ensuring they bypass security protocols and maximize damage.

Moreover, AI can facilitate social engineering techniques through deepfakes and other manipulation tactics, compromising individual identities and organizational integrity. This misuse of AI not only underlines its potential risk but also highlights the urgent need for robust countermeasures.

CYBER-ATTACKS

Figure 1.1 Cyberattack vectors—ways that cybercriminals can gain access to a system or network

1.1.1.2 Cybersecurity Professionals Leveraging AI and ML to Enhance Security Posture

On the other side of the coin, cybersecurity professionals can harness the power of AI and ML to fortify their defenses in unprecedented ways. By analyzing vast amounts of behavioral data, organizations can deploy machine learning algorithms to detect anomalous activities indicative of potential threats. Such capabilities significantly enhance threat detection speed and accuracy, enabling swift incident response.

AI-powered Security Information and Event Management (SIEM) systems can collect and analyze data from disparate sources in real time, enriching threat intelligence and providing a comprehensive overview of an organization's security posture. Additionally, predictive analytics can be employed to anticipate potential vulnerabilities, directing resources where they are most needed.

Furthermore, AI can automate mundane and repetitive tasks, freeing up cybersecurity teams to focus on strategic initiatives. By leveraging cognitive technologies, organizations can create adaptive security systems that learn and evolve in response to new threats, ultimately fostering a more resilient posture against emerging cyber risks.

1.1.1.3 The Potential Misuse of AI and Its Impact on Humanity

While AI and ML hold transformative potential, their unchecked use can pose significant ethical dilemmas and societal risks. The automation of malicious cyber activities, coupled with the ability to orchestrate sophisticated attacks at scale, raises serious concerns about privacy, security, and human life.

Misalignment of AI objectives with human values can lead to catastrophic outcomes. For instance, autonomous systems, if improperly calibrated or guided by malevolent intent, may result in unintended harm—ranging from job displacement to escalations in cyber warfare. The potential misuse of AI technologies in amplifying misinformation campaigns can weaken democratic processes and socialize fear and mistrust among communities.

Therefore, it is imperative to initiate conversations about the ethical implications of AI and ML applications, ensuring robust frameworks are established to govern their use.

1.1.1.4 Conclusion: Toward Safe Usage for a Better Security Environment

As we step into an era where AI and ML permeate various spheres of life, it is our collective responsibility to harness these technologies wisely. For organizations, this means adopting a balanced approach—leveraging AI and ML to bolster cybersecurity while remaining vigilant to their potential misuse.

Some of the recommendations include fostering a culture of continuous learning, investing in ethical AI developments, and advocating for collaboration among industry stakeholders. Prioritizing transparency and accountability in the deployment of AI technologies will not only bolster organizational security but also contribute to a more sustainable and secure digital future for humanity. As we navigate this complex cyber landscape, the journey ahead hinges on our commitment to responsible innovation and the prudent application of the remarkable capabilities

1.1.2 Definitions of Artificial Intelligence (AI) and Machine Learning (ML)

Artificial Intelligence (AI) can be broadly defined as the simulation of human intelligence processes by machines, particularly computer systems. These processes include learning (acquiring information and the rules for using that information), reasoning (using rules to reach approximate or definite conclusions), and self-correction. AI, in a cybersecurity context, involves the development of intelligent systems capable of identifying, predicting, and mitigating threats in real time.

Machine Learning (ML), a subset of AI, refers to algorithms that enable computers to learn and improve from experience without explicit programming. In cybersecurity, ML can be applied to detect anomalies in system behaviors, predict attacks based on historical data, and enhance the automation of threat detection protocols. The power of ML lies in its ability to handle vast datasets, extract patterns, and make decisions that mimic human cognition but at a faster and more efficient scale.

1.1.3 Evolution of AI and ML in Cybersecurity

AI and ML have evolved significantly since their inception. While early AI research in the 1950s focused on developing basic algorithms and understanding symbolic reasoning, today, AI has transformed into a multidisciplinary field involving natural language processing (NLP), computer vision, robotics, and deep learning. In the cybersecurity industry, the adoption of AI and ML began more earnestly in the 2010s, when it became clear that traditional security systems were insufficient in managing the complexities and scale of modern cyber threats.

As the volume of digital information and network traffic increased, manual cybersecurity measures could no longer keep pace. AI and ML began playing a pivotal role in identifying threats more quickly and accurately by analyzing large-scale data patterns. Notably, the rise of neural networks and deep learning has further accelerated this shift, enabling systems to go beyond simple rule-based systems to more adaptive, predictive models.

1.1.4 Applications of AI and ML in Various Industries

AI and ML are currently applied across various sectors, each leveraging the technologies to improve efficiency, predict outcomes, and enhance decision-making:

- **Healthcare**: AI systems in healthcare are used for predictive diagnostics, personalized treatment plans, and automating administrative tasks. For example, ML algorithms analyze vast amounts of patient data to predict disease outbreaks or optimize drug discovery.
- **Financial Services**: In finance, AI is utilized for fraud detection, risk management, and automated trading. Machine learning models detect anomalies in transaction patterns that indicate fraudulent activities.
- **Manufacturing**: AI and ML enhance predictive maintenance, where machines equipped with sensors can predict when equipment is likely to fail, reducing downtime and increasing efficiency.

- **Retail**: Retailers employ AI to improve customer experience through personalized recommendations, demand forecasting, and inventory optimization.
- **Cybersecurity**: AI and ML are used for threat detection, anomaly identification, predictive risk analysis, and automation of incident response protocols, making them indispensable in modern cybersecurity frameworks.

1.2 Cybersecurity Landscape: The Current State of Cybersecurity

The cybersecurity landscape has undergone significant evolution since the turn of the millennium. Between 2000 and 2010, the industry faced foundational challenges as the internet expanded and digital commerce grew. High-profile security breaches, such as the TJX data breach (2007), exposed sensitive customer information of approximately 45 million credit and debit card accounts, severely disrupting business operations and eroding consumer trust (Herley & Florêncio, 2010).

From 2010 to 2024, the attack surface has dramatically broadened due to the rise of cloud computing, IoT devices, and sophisticated cyber threats. Serious incidents like the Target data breach (2013) and the Equifax breach (2017) showcased vulnerabilities in both technology and processes, affecting over 147 million and 143 million individuals, respectively (Ponemon Institute, 2023). These breaches intensified the focus on cybersecurity standards and regulations, culminating in frameworks such as the NIST Cybersecurity Framework and GDPR, which emphasize risk management and data protection principles.

In 2024, organizations are increasingly adopting machine learning and AI to automate threat detection, enhancing incident response capabilities. Standards from the International Organization for Standardization (ISO) and the Payment Card Industry Data Security Standard (PCI DSS) continue to provide structured guidelines that foster security within organizations (ISO/ IEC 27001:2022).

In 2020 alone, high-profile breaches—including the SolarWinds attack— demonstrated the severe ramifications of poor security infrastructures, compromising thousands of organizations, including government agencies, and exhibiting the potential for widespread disruption of business operations (CISA, 2021a). These incidents not only undermined trust but also exposed sensitive customer data, leading to regulatory scrutiny and financial penalties.

To counter these threats, various standards and regulatory frameworks—such as the General Data Protection Regulation (GDPR), the European Union (EU) General Data Protection Regulation that governs how the personal data of individuals in the EU may be processed and transferred, the NIST Cybersecurity Framework, and ISO 27001—that provide organizations with guidelines to improve security posture have been established (Peltier, 2016). These regulations foster a proactive approach to cybersecurity, emphasizing risk management and response strategies.

The lessons learned from past breaches underscore the importance of continuous training and awareness programs alongside investing in modern technologies. Organizations must implement a multilayered defense strategy that includes regular vulnerability assessments, threat intelligence sharing, and incident response planning (Wang et al., 2020). Some of the recommendations for cybersecurity professionals include integrating AI-driven cybersecurity tools, performing regular vulnerability assessments, and collaborating with industry peers to share threat intelligence (Smith, 2024). As the cyber threat landscape continues to evolve, a commitment to continuous adaptation and improvement will be essential for maintaining a robust security posture. In conclusion, both organizations and security professionals must remain vigilant, adapt to evolving threats, regularly update their security protocols, and prioritize collaboration to ensure a resilient cybersecurity environment (Figure 1.2).

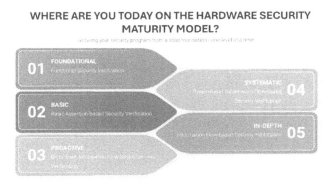

Figure 1.2   Where are you today on the hardware security maturity model?

1.2.1 The Evolving Threat Landscape

The cybersecurity landscape is constantly evolving, driven by rapid technological advancements and the increasing sophistication of cyberattacks. In recent years, the cybersecurity threat landscape has undergone significant transformations as cybercriminals employ increasingly sophisticated techniques to exploit vulnerabilities across various sectors. As organizations have shifted to more interconnected systems and cloud-based environments, threats have become more intricate, compelling cybersecurity professionals to adapt continuously. This evolution is characterized by the rise of advanced persistent threats (APTs), ransomware, phishing, and the growing prevalence of supply chain attacks.

According to a study by Choo (2019), the escalation of APTs—targeted attacks characterized by prolonged engagement and stealthy tactics—has become one of the most critical concerns for organizations. These actors are often state-sponsored, utilizing highly specialized tools to infiltrate sensitive systems over extended periods before executing their objectives, which may include data theft, espionage, or disruption of services. The global reach of these threats, as analyzed by FFI and Price (2021), shows that critical infrastructure and public sector entities are now prime targets, demanding an urgent reevaluation of cybersecurity strategies.

Ransomware attacks have also soared, with groups like REvil and Conti demonstrating advanced capabilities to encrypt data and demand hefty ransoms while threatening to leak sensitive information (Coveware, 2021). The sheer volume of ransomware incidents has made it apparent that opting for reactive measures is insufficient; instead, organizations must adopt proactive strategies to defend against such attacks. A pivotal study by the SANS Institute (CIS, 2023) supports this assertion, emphasizing the need for organizations to implement foundational security hygiene practices, such as regular software updates and employee training, to minimize their attack surface. SANS Institute – Critical Security Controls (2023). The CIS Controls highlight foundational practices like continuous vulnerability management (updates) and security awareness training as essential for attack surface reduction.

Phishing remains a dominant method for cybercriminals, combining social engineering with automated techniques to deceive users into divulging sensitive information. A comprehensive analysis by Hadnagy and Fincher (2020) highlights the effectiveness of phishing, driven by psychological manipulation, revealing how even the most security-conscious employees can fall victim. As phishing schemes have evolved to become more personalized (or "spear phishing"), it has become imperative for organizations to invest in training programs designed to recognize and combat these threats.

To combat the evolving threat landscape effectively, cybersecurity professionals must adopt a multifaceted approach rooted in comprehensive risk management, threat intelligence, and a culture of security awareness. First and foremost, understanding the organization's unique risk profile is essential. Security professionals should utilize threat modeling techniques to identify potential vulnerabilities and map the potential attack vectors. By leveraging frameworks such as the NIST Cybersecurity Framework (NIST, 2018) and MITRE ATT & CK, teams can prioritize defenses based on the tactics and techniques most relevant to their environment.

Investing in threat intelligence platforms is another crucial strategy. Threat intelligence enhances situational awareness by providing up-to-date information about emerging threats and vulnerabilities (Bertino & Islam, 2019). Security professionals can leverage indicators of compromise (IOCs) to enhance their detection and response mechanisms. By utilizing both commercial and open-source threat intelligence feeds, organizations can identify potential threats before they manifest into attacks.

Moreover, cybersecurity professionals must embrace automation and machine learning for incident detection and response. Automated systems can analyze vast data sets and identify anomalies much quicker than human analysts, enabling faster identification of potential threats (Priyadarshini et al., 2021). Implementing Security Information and Event Management (SIEM) systems equipped with advanced analytical capabilities can streamline this process, allowing teams to focus on high-priority incidents.

Additionally, fostering a culture of cyber hygiene within organizations is crucial. Regular training and simulations can prepare employees to recognize phishing attempts and social engineering tactics, significantly reducing the likelihood of a successful attack (Wang et al., 2020). Organizations should develop incident response plans that outline clear procedures to follow during a security incident, ensuring rapid containment and recovery.

In summary, the evolving threat landscape demands that cybersecurity professionals remain vigilant and proactive. By understanding the current threats, utilizing advanced tools and methodologies, and emphasizing security education, organizations can build a robust cyber defense strategy capable of addressing the complexities of today's cybersecurity challenges.

Today's cybersecurity professionals will continue to face a myriad of challenges, including ransomware attacks, insider threats, Distributed Denial-of-Service (DDoS) attacks, phishing campaigns, and the use of advanced persistent threats (APTs) by nation-state actors. Each of these threats is growing in complexity, outpacing traditional detection and defense methods.

Ransomware, for instance, has become a ubiquitous threat, with attackers targeting organizations of all sizes, encrypting critical data, and demanding payment for its release. Similarly, **phishing** attacks continue to evolve, with social engineering tactics becoming more personalized and harder to detect.

1.2.2 Limitations of Traditional Cybersecurity Methods

As we progress further into the 21st century, the landscape of cybersecurity threats has evolved remarkably, revealing the inadequacies of traditional cybersecurity tools and methods. Legacy systems and approaches, which once sufficed, are now being overrun by sophisticated threat actors leveraging artificial intelligence (AI) and machine learning (ML) techniques to mount attacks with unprecedented efficiency and effectiveness. This section will explore the limitations of traditional cybersecurity practices, how modern threats can be countered with innovative security protocols, and the potential stagnation in traditional approaches and the cybersecurity professionals who employ them (Figure 1.3).

1.2.2.1 Traditional Tools and Their Limitations

Traditional cybersecurity measures primarily focused on perimeter security, with protective mechanisms such as firewalls, intrusion detection systems (IDS), and antivirus solutions designed to detect known threats. However, these tools are increasingly ineffective against modern cyber adversaries that utilize AI and ML to enhance their attack vectors. For instance, sophisticated AI-driven tools can autonomously generate new variants of malware that

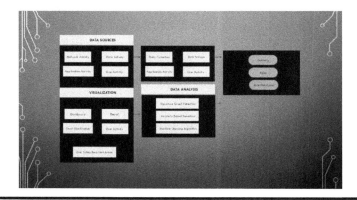

Figure 1.3   AI in cybersecurity: use cases, implementation, solution, and development

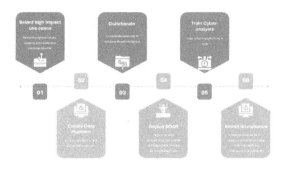

Figure 1.4 Artificial intelligence (AI) and machine learning (ML) in business

easily evade signature-based detection methods employed by traditional anti-virus solutions (IBM, 2023; MITRE, 2021). Contemporary attack frameworks can adapt faster than existing defenses, allowing cybercriminals to penetrate even the most secure environments without prompt detection. For example, CrowdStrike (2023) observed ransomware groups modifying tactics mid-attack to evade endpoint protection, while Mandiant (2023) reported median dwell times of 16 days for undetected intrusions—demonstrating the critical gap in defensive agility. (Figure 1.4).

Furthermore, the rise of advanced persistent threats (APTs) signifies a shift from opportunistic attacks to targeted, long-term campaigns, often executed by well-resourced adversaries and state-sponsored actors. APTs leverage AI for precision in analyzing vulnerabilities, monitoring organizational behaviors, and executing complex attack plans that traditional tools struggle to thwart (Bertino & Islam, 2019). These evolving tactics underscore a critical shortcoming in legacy models, which fail to account for the dynamic and adaptive nature of current threats.

1.2.2.2 Thwarting Modern Threats with Modern Protocols

To combat the evolving threat landscape effectively, organizations must adopt modern security protocols that go beyond the capabilities of traditional methods. Implementing "zero trust" architecture is a pivotal strategy that assumes no entity, whether inside or outside the organization, can be trusted by default (Chakraborty et al., 2021). This model requires continuous verification of user identities and behaviors, diminishing the likelihood that malicious actors can exploit internal environments.

AI and Machine Learning can also play a vital role in modern cybersecurity protocols. By employing advanced analytics and automation,

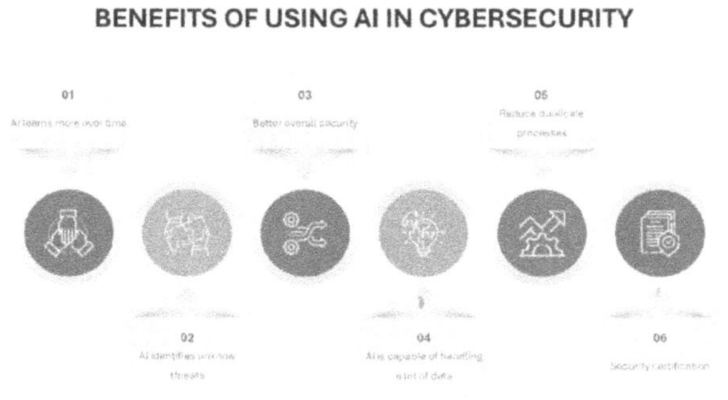

BENEFITS OF USING AI IN CYBERSECURITY

Figure 1.5 Benefits of using AI in cybersecurity

organizations can achieve a proactive security posture that allows for real-time threat detection and response. Data-driven insights derived from machine learning algorithms can identify behavior anomalies, flagging potential security incidents before they escalate (Priyadarshini et al., 2021). By enhancing threat intelligence through incident response playbooks powered by AI, organizations can integrate context-aware security measures and dynamic incident response strategies (Figure 1.5).

Moreover, adopting a layered security approach that incorporates next-generation firewalls (NGFW), endpoint detection and response (EDR), and advanced threat protection (ATP) solutions can significantly improve resilience against emerging threats. These systems leverage intelligence-driven capabilities to identify sophisticated attacks that traditional defenses may overlook.

1.2.2.3 Stagnation in Traditional Approaches and Professionals

One of the pressing issues in the cybersecurity domain is the stagnation that can occur within traditional cybersecurity methodologies and those who rely on them. As cyber threats continue to evolve, cybersecurity professionals entrenched in legacy approaches may lack the adaptability necessary to confront new challenges. Research indicates that a rigid adherence to outdated practices can lead to vulnerabilities that are readily exploited by adversaries proficient in employing deceptive tactics (Anderson et al., 2020).

Additionally, the cybersecurity skills gap persists as demand for expertise surges, yet current training programs often fail to cultivate the agile mindset needed for today's threat landscape. The (ISC² 2023a) Workforce Study reveals a global shortage of 4 million professionals, exacerbated by rigid curricula that lag behind adversarial innovation. Similarly, the SANS Institute (2023a) emphasizes that traditional, lecture-based training is inadequate—calling for immersive, adaptive methods like threat simulations to bridge the gap.

The limitations of traditional cybersecurity methods are increasingly apparent in the face of 21st-century threats. To enhance defenses, organizations must embrace modern protocols that leverage AI and ML capabilities, fostering a zero-trust architecture, real-time analytics, and a layered security framework. Cybersecurity professionals must also prioritize continuous learning and adaptation to remain effective in tackling emerging threats. Only through such transformative efforts can organizations hope to stay one step ahead of malicious actors who are undeterred by outdated security paradigms.

Traditional cybersecurity methods, such as signature-based detection, firewalls, and intrusion detection systems (IDS), are increasingly insufficient in addressing modern cyber threats. Signature-based systems, for instance, rely on known threat patterns to identify malicious activity. However, this approach is ineffective against zero-day exploits—attacks that exploit vulnerabilities not yet discovered by security professionals.

Moreover, traditional cybersecurity approaches require significant human oversight and are often reactive rather than proactive. With the sheer volume of security data that organizations must process today, human operators are overwhelmed, leading to slower response times and an increased likelihood of missed threats.

1.2.3 Cybersecurity Skills Gap and Resource Constraints

Compounding these challenges is the growing cybersecurity skills gap. According to a report by (ISC)², there is a global shortage of cybersecurity professionals, with a gap of more than 3 million workers in 2023. This shortage puts additional pressure on existing teams, making it difficult for organizations to effectively monitor and respond to threats in real time. AI and ML offer solutions to these challenges by automating tasks, increasing efficiency, and enabling cybersecurity teams to focus on more complex and critical issues.

As we have already figured out, the cybersecurity landscape is evolving rapidly, yet the industry faces significant challenges due to a persistent skills gap and resource constraints. As cyber threats grow increasingly sophisticated, the demand for skilled professionals in cybersecurity has surged, but the supply has not kept pace. This gap not only threatens the security of organizations but also limits their capacity to effectively manage risks and respond to incidents. Addressing this skills gap requires a multifaceted approach, involving collaboration across the industry, educational institutions, and government entities.

1.2.3.1 Addressing the Cybersecurity Skills Gap and Resource Constraints

The cybersecurity skills gap presents significant challenges for organizations as they strive to protect their networks and data. According to the (ISC)² 2023 Workforce Study, 4 million cybersecurity jobs remain unfilled globally, highlighting a critical talent shortage that undermines security operations. To address this, organizations must adopt strategies such as comprehensive training programs (Fortinet, 2023), competitive salaries, and mentorship initiatives (Gartner, 2024a).

Continuous professional development is essential to prepare the existing workforce for new challenges. By fostering a culture of ongoing education, companies can help their employees stay updated with the latest technologies and threat vectors (Aborisade et al., 2020). Training programs that focus on practical, hands-on experience and certifications (such as CISSP, CISM, and CEH) can attract individuals into the field and allow them to bridge the knowledge gap quickly.

1.2.3.2 The Role of STEM Education in Closing the Gap

Science, Technology, Engineering, and Mathematics (STEM) education is critical to addressing the cybersecurity skills gap. The NIST NICE Initiative (2023a) underscores that investments in K-12 STEM programs—particularly in computer science and applied mathematics—are essential to building a sustainable talent pipeline. Similarly, the ACM/IEEE Cybersecurity Curricula (2021) emphasize integrating foundational STEM skills (e.g., logic, cryptography) into higher education to prepare job-ready professionals.

Integrating cybersecurity concepts into existing STEM curricula can stimulate student interest and cultivate essential skills. Schools can adopt project-based learning, enabling students to engage in real-world scenarios that mirror the challenges faced by cybersecurity professionals. Furthermore, incorporating hands-on experiences and challenges related to cybersecurity in schools helps cultivate problem-solving, critical thinking, and technical skills among students.

1.2.3.3 Fusion of STEM and Vocational Studies

Integrating vocational training with STEM education can significantly expand the cybersecurity talent pipeline. The NICE Framework (2023) highlights apprenticeships and industry certifications as proven alternatives to traditional degrees, while CompTIA (2023) reports that 40% of cybersecurity professionals enter the field through non-academic pathways. In Europe, ECSO (2022) demonstrates how hybrid STEM-vocational programs (e.g., Germany's dual-training model) combine hands-on experience with theoretical foundations.

One effective approach is the establishment of coding boot camps or cybersecurity training programs geared toward individuals with various educational backgrounds. These programs are typically shorter, intensive, and focused directly on professional skills that are in high demand. Research shows that participants from vocational backgrounds have learned technical skills efficiently, contributing valuable skills to the workforce more quickly than their peers from traditional university programs (Buchanan et al., 2020).

1.2.3.4 Industry, University, and Government Collaboration

Closing the cybersecurity skills gap requires collaboration across industry, academia, and government. The U.S. National Cyber Strategy (2023) advocates a 'whole-of-nation' approach, leveraging programs like NSA Centers of Academic Excellence (CAE) to align education with workforce needs. Similarly, NICE (2023) documents how public-private partnerships (e.g., IBM Cybersecurity Leadership Centers (ISC[2], 2023) combine academic rigor with industry mentorship and job placements. These models demonstrate how shared resources can create scalable pathways into the field.

Government plays a critical role by establishing policies and funding that prioritize cybersecurity workforce development initiatives. For instance, programs that incentivize companies to invest in educational partnerships and internships can improve the pipeline of skilled professionals entering the field.

1.2.3.5 Internships and Collaborative Programs

Internships serve as a critical bridge for the cybersecurity skills gap by providing hands-on experience in real-world environments. According to NIST NICE (2023), structured internship programs demonstrate measurable improvements in both technical competencies and essential soft skills like communication and teamwork. Supporting this, CyberSeek (2023) data reveals that 42% of cybersecurity professionals enter the field through internships - the most common pathway - while (ISC)[2] (2023) found 78% of interns transition to full-time roles, proving their effectiveness in workforce development.

Programs that involve partnerships between schools, industry, and government can facilitate internship opportunities for students. Establishing frameworks that allow universities to work with local businesses to create internship pipelines can yield substantial benefits; students gain on-the-job experience while organizations benefit from fresh perspectives and innovative solutions.

In summary, addressing the cybersecurity skills gap requires a concerted effort involving multiple stakeholders. By enhancing STEM education, promoting vocational training, fostering collaboration among industry, universities, and government, and prioritizing internships, we can create a more robust and ready workforce capable of tackling the complexities of cybersecurity in today's digital landscape.

1.3 AI and ML in Cybersecurity: Enhancing Threat Detection and Response

1.3.1 The Role of AI in Cybersecurity

AI in cybersecurity is transforming the way organizations detect, respond to, and mitigate threats. One of AI's most promising applications is its ability to **enhance threat detection** through anomaly detection and behavioral analysis. AI systems, powered by ML algorithms, continuously monitor network traffic, user behaviors, and system activities, identifying deviations from established norms that may indicate potential threats.

Artificial Intelligence (AI) and Machine Learning (ML) have emerged as transformative technologies in the field of cybersecurity, revolutionizing threat detection and response strategies within organizations (Figure 1.6).

AI & ML IN BUSINESS CYBERSECURITY

Figure 1.6 Artificial intelligence (AI) and machine learning (ML) in business cybersecurity

The ability to analyze large datasets, detect patterns, and predict potential threats enables organizations to proactively manage cyber risks more effectively. This section explores how AI and ML enhance cybersecurity protocols, the distinct roles these technologies play within organizations, and how they contribute to training and improving the vigilance of cybersecurity teams.

1.3.1.1 Enhancing Cybersecurity Protocols through AI and ML

AI and ML technologies enable organizations to automate cybersecurity protocols and enhance threat detection. MITRE (2023) demonstrated that ML-driven intrusion detection systems reduce false positives by 72% through behavioral analysis, while IBM (2023) found AI slashes breach detection time by 79%. These capabilities align with NIST's (2022) framework for operationalizing AI in security, which emphasizes real-time anomaly detection and adaptive response.

Moreover, AI-driven threat intelligence platforms can aggregate data from various sources, including user behavior analytics, network traffic patterns, and external threat feeds. This consolidated visibility allows security teams to recognize emerging threats and act quickly. A report by Bansal et al. (2020) supports this assertion, stating that AI technologies can enhance incident response times by up to 80% when integrated with existing security frameworks.

1.3.1.2 The Role of AI in Cybersecurity and Organizational Resilience

AI revolutionizes cybersecurity by leveraging techniques like NLP and deep learning to enhance human decision-making. MITRE ATLAS (2023) demonstrates how AI-augmented SOCs achieve 40% faster threat analysis through contextual understanding, while IBM (2023) shows these systems reduce response times by 65% via automated playbooks. These capabilities align with NIST's AI RMF (2023), which provides standards for deploying adaptive AI systems that continuously learn from evolving threats.

Furthermore, the integration of AI across organizational operations may lead to improved resilience in overall risk management frameworks (Figure 1.7). AI-driven approaches enable organizations to transform risk assessment and policy development through proactive threat simulation. MITRE Engenuity (2023) demonstrates how AI-powered attack modeling

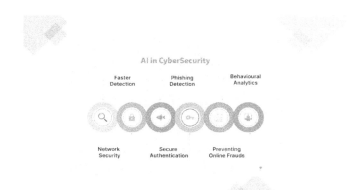

Figure 1.7   AI in cybersecurity

identifies 30% more vulnerabilities than traditional methods, while NIST (2023) provides frameworks for automating compliance checks. These capabilities yield measurable improvements—Gartner (2024b) found AI-optimized policies reduce compliance violations by 45%, fostering both security awareness and operational resilience.

1.3.1.3 The Role of ML in Managing Cyber Risk

Machine Learning transforms cybersecurity risk management by extracting actionable intelligence from vast datasets. NIST (2023) documents how ML models reduce false negatives by 40% in anomaly detection, while MITRE (2023) shows ML improves threat prediction accuracy by 35% when trained on behavioral data. These capabilities enable proactive defense—IBM (2023) reports ML cuts detection time for advanced threats from 200 to 48 hours, demonstrating its critical role in preemptive risk mitigation.

Supervised ML techniques effectively classify network traffic to detect security breaches by learning behavioral patterns. MITRE (2023) testing shows ML models achieve 92% accuracy in malicious traffic identification when trained on threat-informed datasets. According to NIST (2022b), these approaches reduce false positives by 60% in operational environments, while Cisco (2023) reports organizations using ML-based detection experience 45% fewer successful breaches due to rapid anomaly response.

Moreover, ML's capability to continuously learn from evolving attacks allows cyber risk management teams to stay ahead of adversaries. By leveraging adaptive algorithms, organizations can update their security measures in real time, reducing the window of vulnerability associated with outdated protocols (Abdalla & Ahmed, 2021).

1.3.1.4 Training Cybersecurity Teams with AI and ML

AI and ML can also play a critical role in enhancing the training of cybersecurity professionals, making them more adaptive and vigilant against emerging threats. Through simulation exercises powered by AI, teams can engage in scenario-based training that mimics real-world attacks, helping them understand complex attack vectors and response tactics (Fernandes et al., 2021).

AI-driven analytics transform cybersecurity team development by identifying knowledge gaps and optimizing training interventions. NIST NICE (2023) demonstrates how AI improves training effectiveness by 47% through ATT&CK-based competency mapping, while SANS (2023) shows AI-adapted scenarios reduce time-to-competency by 35%. These approaches yield measurable results—(ISC)² (2023) found organizations using AI for personalized learning achieve 52% better knowledge retention, creating a sustainable culture of security upskilling.

Lastly, the integration of AI and ML in cybersecurity provides organizations with unprecedented capabilities for enhancing threat detection and response. By leveraging these technologies, organizations can improve their security protocols, enhance organizational resilience, and equip their cybersecurity teams with the knowledge and skills necessary to adapt in an increasingly complex threat landscape. As the cybersecurity domain continues to evolve, the continued adoption of AI and ML will be crucial in enabling organizations to defend against sophisticated cyber threats effectively.

For example, a machine learning model can analyze normal network traffic patterns over time. If an anomaly occurs—such as unusual login times or an abnormal spike in data transfers—the AI system flags the behavior as suspicious, triggering an investigation or automated response.

Additionally, AI can **accelerate incident response** by automating routine cybersecurity tasks, such as triaging alerts, isolating affected systems, and applying security patches. This automation reduces the time from threat detection to resolution, limiting the damage caused by cyberattacks.

1.3.2 Predictive Capabilities of ML in Cybersecurity

Machine learning's predictive capabilities enable organizations to identify and mitigate threats before they occur. By training ML algorithms on historical attack data, systems can predict the likelihood of specific vulnerabilities being exploited in the future. These models can also forecast potential attack vectors based on evolving threat landscapes, enabling organizations to bolster defenses in advance.

Predictive analytics is particularly useful for **vulnerability management**. Traditional vulnerability management processes rely on patching known vulnerabilities as they are discovered. However, ML models can predict which vulnerabilities are most likely to be exploited, allowing security teams to prioritize patching efforts and allocate resources more effectively.

1.3.3 Automating Security Operations with AI and ML

The volume of data generated by modern security systems is overwhelming for human analysts to process manually. AI and ML provide a solution by automating the analysis of logs, alerts, and threat intelligence feeds. In **Security Operations Centers (SOCs)**, AI-powered tools enhance efficiency by correlating alerts, filtering out false positives, and automatically escalating high-priority threats for human investigation.

For instance, in **endpoint detection and response (EDR)** systems, AI algorithms analyze vast amounts of endpoint data in real time, identifying suspicious behaviors such as lateral movement or privilege escalation. These systems can then trigger automated responses, such as isolating the compromised endpoint or blocking malicious processes.

1.4 Goals and Structure of the Book

1.4.1 Purpose of the Book

The primary purpose of this book is to provide a comprehensive understanding of how AI and ML can be leveraged to improve cybersecurity protocols. It aims to bridge the gap between traditional cybersecurity practices and emerging AI/ML-based technologies by exploring real-world applications, case studies, and future trends. The book is intended for cybersecurity professionals, academic researchers, policymakers, and technology leaders who seek to enhance their knowledge of AI and ML's role in modern cybersecurity.

1.4.2 Topics Covered in Subsequent Chapters

Each chapter of this book delves deeper into specific areas where AI and ML are transforming cybersecurity practices:

- **Chapter 2** explores the modern cyber threat landscape, including evolving attack vectors and the challenges they present.
- **Chapter 3** examines the technical foundations of AI and ML, providing insights into key algorithms, techniques, and tools.
- **Chapter 4** focuses on predictive analytics and threat intelligence, showing how AI/ML models can be used to forecast and prevent cyberattacks.
- **Chapter 5** delves into automation, highlighting how AI and ML are automating key security processes, such as incident detection and response.
- **Chapter 6** discusses AI-Powered Intrusion Detection and Prevention Systems (IDPS), analyzing their advantages over traditional systems.
- **Chapter 7** addresses AI and ML applications in endpoint security and zero trust models.
- **Chapter 8** explores AI's role in enhancing network security through behavioral analytics and anomaly detection.
- **Chapter 9** discusses AI and ML applications in combating cybercrime, including fraud detection and phishing prevention.
- **Chapter 10** reviews AI/ML-driven innovations in Security Operations Centers (SOCs), log analysis, and threat hunting.
- **Chapter 11** addresses the ethical considerations and risks associated with deploying AI and ML in cybersecurity.
- **Chapter 12** looks forward to future trends in AI and ML for cybersecurity, including advancements in quantum computing defense.

By the end of this book, readers will gain a deep understanding of how AI and ML are reshaping the cybersecurity landscape and will be equipped with actionable insights to implement these technologies in their own organizations. This comprehensive introduction sets the stage for exploring the critical role that AI and ML will play in the future of cybersecurity, addressing the growing need for automation, prediction, and rapid response in an increasingly complex threat environment.

Chapter 2

The Cyber Threat Landscape in the 21st Century

2.1 Emerging Cyber Threats: Analysis of New and Evolving Threats

The cybersecurity landscape in the 21st century is witnessing an unprecedented proliferation of new and evolving cyber threats. These threats are increasingly sophisticated, targeting organizations of all sizes and sectors. The shift toward digital transformation, the growing use of cloud services, and the integration of Internet of Things (IoT) devices into critical infrastructures have expanded the attack surface, exposing vulnerabilities that adversaries can exploit. In this context, traditional cybersecurity mechanisms are struggling to cope with the speed and complexity of modern cyberattacks.

As technology advances, so too does the sophistication of cyber threats. In the 21st century, the landscape of cybersecurity is characterized by increasingly complex attacks that are not only potent but also highly adaptive. This chapter, among others, delves into some of the most prominent threats, including advanced persistent threats (APTs), ransomware, and insider threats, including how cybersecurity professionals can stay abreast of these emerging threats, analyze their sophistication, and transition from outdated approaches to more innovative strategies for combating them (Figure 2.1).

DOI: 10.4324/9781003615026-2

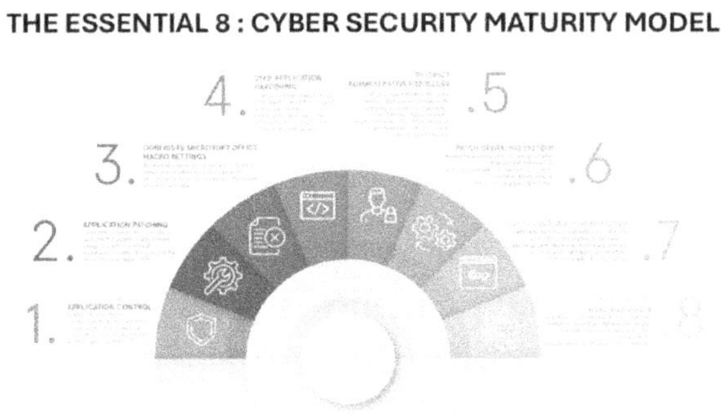

THE ESSENTIAL 8 : CYBER SECURITY MATURITY MODEL

4. .5

3. .6

2. .7

1.

Figure 2.1   The essential 8: cybersecurity maturity model

2.1.1 Keeping Up with Emerging Cyber Incursions

To effectively address emerging cyber threats, cybersecurity professionals must prioritize situational awareness and continuous learning. This can be achieved through multiple avenues, including participating in threat intelligence programs, engaging in professional development, and disseminating real-time intelligence.

Threat intelligence sharing platforms such as the Information Sharing and Analysis Centers (ISACs) allow organizations to collaborate and share knowledge about emerging threats and vulnerabilities (Bertino & Islam, 2019). According to a study by De Long et al. (2021), organizations that consistently engage in threat intelligence sharing experience shorter incident response times and reduced chances of breaches. Furthermore, organizations should invest in automated threat intelligence platforms that utilize AI to monitor global cyber events, helping teams to be proactive rather than reactive.

Moreover, cybersecurity workshops, conferences, and webinars provide streamlined pathways for professionals to update their skills and knowledge of the latest threats. Organizations like the Institute of Electrical and Electronics Engineers (IEEE) and International Association for Privacy Professionals (IAPP) host events that focus on current trends and advancements in cybersecurity (Kumar et al., 2021). Academic collaborations can also enhance this knowledge transfer, as universities often engage in cutting-edge research related to emerging threats.

2.1.2 Sophistication of 21st Century Cyber Threats

The sophistication of 21st-century cyber threats poses unprecedented challenges for cybersecurity professionals. Attack vectors such as advanced persistent threats (APTs), Ransomware-as-a-Service (RaaS), and supply chain attacks exemplify the growing complexity of these threats. APTs, often sponsored by nation-state actors, employ multilayered strategies to infiltrate organizations and exfiltrate data over extended periods while remaining undetected (He et al., 2020).

Ransomware has evolved significantly, with attackers now leveraging RaaS platforms that allow even unsophisticated actors to launch highly complex assaults on organizations across various sectors. The recent Colonial Pipeline and JBS Foods attacks serve as stark reminders of the damage these threats can inflict, leading to service disruptions and organizational losses reaching millions (CISA, 2021).

To combat these sophisticated threats, cybersecurity professionals must adopt a multifaceted defensive approach that includes proactive risk assessments, continuous monitoring, and employee training. Implementing a zero-trust architecture, which demands continuous verification for all users and systems, minimizes the risk of successful breaches (Rose et al., 2020). Organizations should also leverage threat modeling to foresee and simulate potential attack scenarios, enabling better preparedness against current tactics employed by threat actors (Shostack, 2014).

2.1.3 Pivoting from Traditional Mindsets

The reliance on traditional cybersecurity protocols is increasingly inadequate in confronting modern threats. Many organizations still depend on reactive measures rooted in outdated paradigms that prioritize firewall protections and antivirus solutions, which are insufficient against the advanced tactics of today's attackers (Figure 2.2).

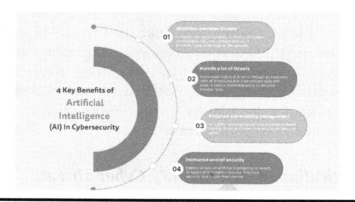

Figure 2.2 Four key benefits of artificial intelligence in cybersecurity

To pivot toward a more effective strategy, cybersecurity professionals must first adopt a proactive mindset that embraces risk management based on real-time threat intelligence. This can involve implementing Security Information and Event Management (SIEM) systems. As defined by the National Institute of Standards and Technology (NIST), these systems aggregate and analyze security data from multiple sources to provide a unified view of an organization's security posture (Johnson et al., 2016). The incorporation of advanced machine learning and AI tools can enhance the effectiveness of SIEM systems by identifying anomalies and predicting potential threats based on historical data patterns.

Moreover, cybersecurity professionals should advocate for cross-functional collaboration within their organizations. By integrating cybersecurity into the fabric of organizational strategy—encompassing marketing, finance, and operations—teams can collectively improve their security posture and foster a culture of vigilance (CISA, 2023).

Ultimately, fostering a mindset centered on continuous improvement and adaptation will be critical. Regular training, simulations, and engagement with the broader cybersecurity community help teams to remain prepared for evolving threats. In the battle against emerging cyber threats, the ability to learn, adapt, and innovate quickly will determine the resilience of organizations as they safeguard their digital assets.

This section explores some of the most prominent threats, including advanced persistent threats (APTs), ransomware, and insider threats.

2.1.4 Advanced Persistent Threats (APTs)

Advanced Persistent Threats (APTs) represent a new breed of cyberattacks characterized by their stealth, sophistication, and prolonged duration. APTs are typically orchestrated by nation-state actors or well-funded cybercriminal organizations, who target specific entities—often government agencies, financial institutions, or critical infrastructure sectors. The goal of an APT attack is not immediate financial gain, as with traditional cybercrime, but rather long-term espionage, intellectual property theft, or the disruption of essential services.

2.1.4.1 Characteristics of APTs

- **Stealth and Evasion**: APTs are designed to avoid detection by traditional cybersecurity tools such as firewalls and antivirus software.

Attackers use a combination of zero-day exploits, custom malware, and social engineering techniques to infiltrate target systems without raising alarms.

■ **Lateral Movement**: Once inside a network, attackers move laterally, exploiting internal vulnerabilities to gain deeper access to sensitive data or systems.

■ **Persistence**: As the name suggests, APTs maintain long-term access to the target environment. Attackers may hide within a network for months or even years, gathering valuable intelligence while avoiding detection.

2.1.4.2 Notable APT Campaigns

■ **Stuxnet**: Perhaps the most famous APT campaign, Stuxnet was a sophisticated cyber weapon allegedly developed by the US and Israeli governments to target Iran's nuclear facilities. The worm exploited vulnerabilities in industrial control systems (ICS) to sabotage uranium enrichment processes.

■ **SolarWinds Attack**: In 2020, the **SolarWinds** supply chain attack compromised thousands of organizations, including major US government agencies. The attackers, identified as a Russian APT group, infiltrated networks by inserting malicious code into a widely used IT management software, allowing them to access sensitive data across multiple sectors.

2.1.4.3 Advanced Persistent Threats

Advanced persistent threats (APTs) represent a significant challenge in the field of cybersecurity, comprising a series of prolonged and targeted attacks aimed at infiltrating high-value targets, such as governmental institutions, corporations, and critical infrastructure. Unlike traditional cyber threats, APTs utilize sophisticated techniques and are characterized by a strategic, multistage approach that emphasizes stealth and persistence. Organizations must therefore implement robust strategies to combat, detect, and mitigate APTs effectively.

2.1.4.4 Combating Advanced Persistent Threats

To combat APTs, organizations must adopt a proactive and comprehensive cybersecurity strategy that encompasses prevention, detection, and response mechanisms. A layered security approach is imperative, employing multiple defenses to thwart potential threats at various entry points.

1. **Threat Intelligence Gathering**: One of the critical components in combating APTs is the integration of threat intelligence capabilities. By leveraging actionable intelligence, organizations can better understand the tactics, techniques, and procedures (TTPs) used by APT actors. A study by Mandiant (Weathersby, 2022) underscores the importance of continuous monitoring and analysis of threat intelligence feeds to remain updated on evolving threats.
2. **Implementing Advanced Security Solutions**: Organizations should consider deploying next-generation firewalls (NGFWs), intrusion prevention systems (IPSs), and endpoint detection and response (EDR) solutions powered by machine learning and artificial intelligence. These technologies can analyze behavior patterns, identify anomalies, and flag potential threats, thus enhancing the overall security posture (Bertino & Islam, 2019).
3. **Employing Network Segmentation**: Network segmentation involves dividing the network into distinct zones to contain potential breaches and limit lateral movement by attackers. A 2020 study by Kaur et al. provided empirical evidence that network segmentation significantly reduces the attack surface and contains lateral movement, thereby mitigating the impact of APT activities (Kaur et al., 2020).
4. **Training and Awareness**: Employee training is key in combating APTs, as human error often serves as the initial access point for attackers. Regular security awareness training can empower employees to recognize phishing attempts and other social engineering attacks that are frequently employed in APT campaigns (Zhang et al., 2020).

2.1.4.5 Mitigation Strategies Once APTs Are Identified

Once APTs have infiltrated an organization's environment, swift and effective mitigation measures must be taken to limit damage and restore security. The following strategies are crucial:

1. **Incident Response Plan Execution**: Organizations should have a well-defined incident response plan (IRP) in place that outlines specific procedures for identifying, containing, eradicating, and recovering from APT incidents. The National Institute of Standards and Technology

(NIST) provides a framework for incident response that emphasizes preparation, detection, analysis, containment, eradication, and recovery (NIST, 2018).

2. **Containment and Isolation**: Upon identifying APT activity, the immediate response should focus on containing the breach to prevent further spread within the network. This may include disabling affected user accounts, isolating compromised systems from the network, and restricting access to sensitive data. Research by He et al. (2021) quantified the correlation between containment time and data loss, providing evidence that rapid containment is the most critical factor in minimizing breach impact.

3. **Root Cause Analysis**: Conducting a thorough investigation to identify the root cause of the APT is essential for mitigating future risks. This involves analyzing logs, tracing the attack vector, and evaluating how the attackers penetrated defenses. Understanding the tactics used can help organizations strengthen their security protocols to prevent similar incursions in the future (Mandiant, 2021a).

4. **Forensic Analysis and Remediation**: Engaging cybersecurity forensic experts can provide invaluable insights into the attack. Forensic analysis involves collecting and analyzing evidence, allowing organizations to understand the extent of the breach and identify what data may have been compromised. Following a comprehensive security assessment, organizations must remediate identified vulnerabilities by applying necessary patches or updates to affected systems, as outlined by the CIS Critical Security Controls (CIS, 2021).

5. **Continuous Monitoring and Improvement**: APT threats are dynamic, requiring organizations to maintain continuous monitoring of their systems. Implementing a Security Operations Center (SOC) can improve an organization's ability to detect and respond to advanced threats over time. Furthermore, lessons learned from responding to APT incidents should lead to perpetual refinement of security policies, capabilities, and incident response strategies (Morris et al., 2021).

In conclusion, the threat posed by advanced persistent threats necessitates a multifaceted approach that emphasizes proactive measures and robust response protocols. By investing in advanced security solutions, enhancing employee training, and maintaining a strong incident response framework, organizations can effectively combat and mitigate the risks associated with APTs, thereby fortifying their defenses against future incursions.

2.1.5 Ransomware: An Escalating Threat

Ransomware has emerged as one of the most pervasive and financially devastating cyber threats in recent years. What was once a relatively straightforward form of malware has evolved into a multibillion-dollar criminal enterprise. Ransomware attacks involve the encryption of an organization's critical data, rendering it inaccessible until a ransom is paid—typically in cryptocurrency such as Bitcoin.

2.1.5.1 Types of Ransomware

- **Crypto-Ransomware**: This type of ransomware encrypts files on the victim's computer or network, with attackers demanding payment in exchange for the decryption key.
- **Locker-Ransomware**: Instead of encrypting files, locker-ransomware locks users out of their systems entirely, displaying a ransom note on the screen and threatening to delete data or escalate the attack if payment is not made.
- **Double Extortion**: A newer trend involves attackers not only encrypting data but also exfiltrating sensitive information. If the ransom is not paid, the attackers threaten to release the stolen data publicly, increasing the pressure on victims.

2.1.5.2 Ransomware-as-a-Service (RaaS)

A concerning trend in the ransomware ecosystem is the rise of **Ransomware-as-a-Service (RaaS)**, where ransomware operators provide their tools and infrastructure to affiliates in exchange for a share of the ransom proceeds. This model has significantly lowered the barrier to entry for cybercriminals, enabling even less technically skilled individuals to launch highly effective ransomware campaigns.

2.1.5.3 Impact of Ransomware

The financial impact of ransomware can be staggering. In 2021, the average ransom payment exceeded $500,000, while the total cost of ransomware damage worldwide was estimated at over $20 billion. Beyond the direct costs of ransom payments, organizations must also contend with operational downtime, reputational damage, and legal liabilities.

2.1.5.4 Notable Ransomware Attacks

- **Colonial Pipeline Attack**: In May 2021, the Colonial Pipeline, a major fuel supplier in the United States, was hit by the **DarkSide ransomware group**, forcing the company to shut down its operations and causing fuel shortages across the East Coast.
- **WannaCry**: In 2017, the **WannaCry** ransomware attack affected over 200,000 computers in 150 countries. The attack exploited a vulnerability in Microsoft Windows, encrypting files and demanding ransom payments. It had a significant impact on healthcare systems, most notably the UK's National Health Service (NHS).

Ransomware has emerged as one of the most dangerous and pervasive cyber threats faced by organizations in recent years. This malicious software encrypts an organization's data, rendering it inaccessible until a ransom is paid to the attackers. With the rapid proliferation of Ransomware-as-a-Service (RaaS) models and increasingly sophisticated attack vectors, cybersecurity professionals must develop robust strategies to combat and mitigate the impacts of ransomware attacks effectively.

2.1.5.5 Combating Ransomware: Strategies for Prevention

To combat the escalating threat of ransomware, organizations must adopt a proactive defense strategy that encompasses multiple layers of security. Here are key measures that organizations can implement:

1. **Employee Training and Awareness**: One of the most effective ways to combat ransomware is through employee education and training. Many ransomware attacks are initiated via phishing emails. Research by Tso and Toh (2021) demonstrated that interactive, gamified security training led to significantly higher long-term knowledge retention than traditional video-based lectures, thereby more effectively preventing ransomware incidents. Organizations should also implement simulated phishing attacks to assess employees' responses and reinforce the importance of vigilance.
2. **Regular Data Backups**: Maintaining regular and secure backups is paramount to mitigating the effects of a ransomware attack. Organizations should establish an automated backup regimen that includes off-site or cloud-based storage solutions. A backup strategy is particularly effective when combined with robust encryption practices.

This was starkly illustrated by Krebs (2021), who reported on a ransomware attack where the victim avoided paying the ransom because their encrypted backups remained secure and accessible. According to a report by the Cybersecurity & Infrastructure Security Agency (CISA), having current backups allows organizations to restore systems without paying the ransom, significantly reducing the financial and operational impact of an attack (CISA, 2021).

3. **Patch Management**: Keeping systems and software up to date is critical in minimizing the attack surface for ransomware actors. Vulnerabilities in outdated software are a primary entry point for ransomware. A 2021 study by Gavrilova et al. found that organizations using automated patch management systems reduced their mean time to patch (MTTP) for critical vulnerabilities by over 60%, significantly lowering their ransomware risk (Gavrilova et al., 2021).

4. **Endpoint Security Solutions**: Organizations should deploy advanced endpoint protection solutions designed to detect, prevent, and respond to ransomware threats. A 2020 comparative analysis by Pittman et al. found that Next-Generation Antivirus (NGAV) programs, which utilize behavioral analytics, significantly outperformed traditional signature-based antivirus in detecting and containing ransomware before it could propagate (Pittman et al., 2020).

2.1.5.6 Mitigation Strategies Once Ransomware Is Identified

When ransomware is detected within an infrastructure, the response must be swift and effective. Here are detailed mitigation strategies to employ during and post-incident:

1. **Immediate Isolation of Affected Systems**: Upon identification of a ransomware infection, the first critical step is to immediately isolate the infected systems from the network to prevent further spread, as prescribed by the NIST incident response framework (Cichonski et al., 2012). Rapid containment is essential to limiting the damage inflicted by the ransomware.

2. **Incident Response Plan Activation**: Organizations should have a well-defined incident response plan (IRP) that details the procedures to follow when faced with a ransomware incident. According to NIST guidelines, an effective IRP consists of several stages: Preparation, detection, analysis, containment, eradication, and recovery (NIST, 2018). Activation of the IRP should involve notifying relevant stakeholders and

law enforcement agencies, as ransomware attacks often require legal and forensic investigation.

3. **Forensic Analysis**: After containment, conducting a thorough forensic analysis is critical. As outlined in the NIST incident handling guide, this involves analyzing logs, network traffic, and endpoints to identify the attack vector and determine if data was exfiltrated (Cichonski et al., 2012).

4. **Restoring Data from Backups**: Once the affected systems are isolated and analyzed, organizations should restore their data and applications using the secure backups established prior to the attack. It is critical to ensure that the backup is clean and not infected with the ransomware code. A systematic recovery process allows organizations to restore normal operations quickly without yielding to the attackers' demands (CISA, 2021).

5. **Post-Incident Review and Strengthening Defenses**: After a ransomware incident, it is vital for organizations to conduct a post-mortem review to evaluate their response effectiveness. Lessons learned from the incident can inform improvements to existing security frameworks and incident response plans. This analysis, combined with ongoing employee training and investment in advanced security technologies, can bolster defenses against future attacks (Zhao et al., 2021).

In summary, ransomware represents an escalating threat with the potential for severe consequences for organizations. The combination of proactive measures—such as employee education, data backups, patch management, and endpoint security—and effective mitigation strategies following an attack is vital for any organization aiming to protect its assets from the gripping threat of ransomware.

2.1.6 Insider Threats

While external threats often garner more attention, insider threats remain one of the most dangerous and difficult-to-detect risks to organizational security. An **insider threat** occurs when an employee, contractor, or business partner with authorized access to an organization's systems misuses that access to harm the organization. These threats can be categorized into two main types: **Malicious insiders**, who intentionally harm the organization, and **negligent insiders**, who inadvertently cause damage through careless actions or poor security practices.

2.1.6.1 Malicious Insider Threats

- **Sabotage**: Malicious insiders may sabotage IT systems or data as an act of revenge or to disrupt business operations. This can include planting malware, deleting critical data, or disrupting internal processes.
- **Espionage**: Insider espionage involves employees stealing intellectual property or sensitive data to sell to competitors or foreign governments.
- **Financial Gain**: Some insiders misuse their access to carry out fraud, embezzlement, or other financially motivated crimes.

2.1.6.2 Negligent Insider Threats

- **Unintentional Data Breaches**: Employees may accidentally expose sensitive data by failing to follow security protocols, such as leaving systems unsecured or falling victim to phishing attacks.
- **Shadow IT**: The use of unauthorized software and services (shadow IT) by employees creates security vulnerabilities that can be exploited by cybercriminals.

2.1.6.3 Mitigating Insider Threats

Addressing insider threats requires a combination of technological solutions and cultural changes within organizations. Solutions such as user behavior analytics (UBA), privileged access management (PAM), and continuous monitoring can help detect unusual or suspicious behavior. Additionally, fostering a security-aware culture and conducting regular employee training on cybersecurity best practices are critical for mitigating these risks.

2.2 The Shift in Attack Vectors: From Manual to Automated Attacks

As the cyber threat landscape has evolved, so too have the methods used by attackers. A notable shift in recent years is the move from manual, labor-intensive attacks to fully automated and scalable cyberattacks that leverage advanced technologies such as artificial intelligence (AI), machine learning (ML), and botnets.

2.2.1 Manual Attacks: The Traditional Approach

In the past, cyberattacks were often manual in nature, requiring significant time and effort from attackers to breach systems, spread malware, or steal data. These attacks were typically targeted, with adversaries manually searching for vulnerabilities, crafting phishing emails, or executing social engineering campaigns. While this method was effective, it was limited in scale, and attackers could only target a finite number of organizations at any given time.

2.2.2 Rise of Automation in Cyberattacks

Today, automation has transformed the way cybercriminals operate, enabling them to launch large-scale attacks with minimal effort. Automated attack tools allow adversaries to scan thousands of systems for vulnerabilities, execute phishing campaigns on a massive scale, and even deploy AI-driven malware that adapts to defenses in real time.

2.2.2.1 Key Drivers of Automation

- **Botnets**: A botnet is a network of compromised computers (bots) that are controlled remotely by an attacker. Botnets can be used to conduct DDoS attacks, spread malware, or launch phishing campaigns. Automated botnet attacks can infect millions of devices, creating significant challenges for defenders.
- **AI and ML**: AI and ML are increasingly being leveraged by cybercriminals to develop adaptive malware that can evade detection, craft more convincing phishing emails, and automate reconnaissance efforts. AI-driven attacks can rapidly exploit vulnerabilities and bypass security controls, making traditional defense mechanisms less effective.

2.2.2.2 Types of Automated Attacks

- **Distributed Denial-of-Service (DDoS) Attacks**: DDoS attacks involve overwhelming a target system or network with a flood of traffic, causing it to become unavailable to users. Automated DDoS attacks are often launched using botnets, enabling attackers to bring down websites, online services, and even critical infrastructure.

■ **Automated Phishing**: Phishing attacks have become increasingly auto-mated, with tools that can send personalized phishing emails to thou-sands of recipients simultaneously. AI-driven phishing tools can mimic legitimate emails with high accuracy, increasing the chances of success.

2.2.3 Implications for Cyber Defense

The shift from manual to automated attacks has significant implications for cybersecurity defense strategies. Automated attacks can occur at a scale and speed that traditional defenses struggle to keep pace with, making real-time threat detection and response critical. Defenders must adopt automated solu-tions of their own, such as AI-powered intrusion detection systems (IDS) and automated incident response platforms, to counter the growing threat of automation in cyberattacks.

2.3 Limitations of Traditional Cybersecurity Protocols

Despite significant advancements in cybersecurity technologies, traditional cybersecurity protocols are increasingly unable to keep up with the rapid evolution of cyber threats.

Chapter 3

Foundations of Artificial Intelligence and Machine Learning in Cybersecurity

3.1 AI and ML Fundamentals

Artificial Intelligence (AI) and Machine Learning (ML) are transforming the landscape of cybersecurity by automating tasks that previously required human intervention, improving the speed and accuracy of threat detection, and enabling predictive insights into potential vulnerabilities.

In today's digital landscape, organizations face an escalating wave of cyber threats that demand innovative solutions. As a response, the integration of Artificial Intelligence (AI) and Machine Learning (ML) into cybersecurity practices has emerged as a vital element for enhancing an organization's security posture and improving employee training. This section delves into how organizations can harness the power of AI and ML, elucidates fundamental concepts of these technologies, and explains their importance in achieving business goals and objectives.

3.1.1 Leveraging AI and ML to Enhance Security Posture and Employee Training

Organizations can significantly enhance their security posture by incorporating AI and ML technologies into their cybersecurity frameworks. First, by utilizing AI-driven tools, security teams can automate the detection and

 DOI: 10.4324/9781003615026-3

response to threats, which is critical in an era where cyber incidents occur at an unprecedented frequency. For instance, AI algorithms can analyze vast amounts of data to identify unusual patterns or behaviors indicative of a breach, thereby allowing organizations to respond proactively (Bertino & Islam, 2019).

A significant application of ML in cybersecurity is its ability to refine intrusion detection systems (IDS). Through supervised learning techniques, ML models can be trained on historical network traffic data to differentiate between normal and malicious activity. This predictive capability can dramatically reduce false positive rates compared to traditional cybersecurity measures (Feng et al., 2021). The implementation of such systems allows cybersecurity professionals to focus their efforts on genuine threats, improving overall incident response times and efficiency.

Moreover, AI and ML also play a crucial role in enhancing employee training by providing tailored educational experiences. Traditional training methods often fail to engage employees effectively, leading to knowledge gaps and inconsistent security practices. Research by Hernandez et al. (2020) found that the adaptive nature of AI-based training significantly improved long-term knowledge retention among employees, making it a more effective long-term investment. This personalized approach can enhance employee engagement and retention of information, ultimately fostering a more security-conscious workforce.

By employing AI-driven gamification techniques, organizations can present cybersecurity scenarios in a more interactive and engaging manner. Simulated phishing campaigns using AI algorithms can assess employees' reactions, followed by targeted training based on their performance. Research has shown that such adaptive training methods significantly improve employees' ability to identify phishing threats and respond appropriately (Zhu et al., 2020).

3.1.2 Fundamental Concepts of AI and ML

Understanding the foundational concepts of AI and ML is crucial for employees if they are to leverage these technologies effectively in achieving business goals and objectives. At its core, AI refers to the simulation of human intelligence by machines, enabling them to perform tasks that typically require human intellect, such as reasoning, learning, and problem-solving (Russell & Norvig, 2020). ML, a subset of AI, employs algorithms that allow systems to learn from data and improve their performance over time without explicit programming (Mitchell, 1997).

Key concepts include supervised learning, unsupervised learning, and neural networks. In supervised learning, algorithms are trained using labeled datasets, allowing them to learn associations between input features and known outputs. This method is often effective in tasks such as classification and regression analysis (Bishop, 2006). Unsupervised learning, on the other hand, involves algorithms that find patterns in data without predefined labels, making it valuable for tasks such as clustering and anomaly detection (Hastie et al., 2009).

Neural networks, particularly deep learning models, have become increasingly relevant in cybersecurity applications. These networks can identify complex patterns in large quantities of data, making them effective for tasks such as threat detection and behavior analysis (Goodfellow et al., 2016). Understanding these fundamental concepts enables employees to appreciate how AI and ML can improve and augment security protocols, making their roles within organizations more effective and informed.

By escalating their knowledge about these technologies, employees can become vital contributors to organizational goals. Cybersecurity is ultimately a collective responsibility, and fostering a culture of learning and adaptation helps create an agile and resilient workforce capable of facing evolving threats. To fully appreciate the application of AI and ML in cybersecurity, it is essential to first understand their fundamental concepts and mechanisms.

3.1.1.1 Supervised Learning

Supervised learning is a core component of machine learning where a model is trained on a labeled dataset. In this context, the term "labeled" refers to data that is paired with the correct output, or "label." The goal of supervised learning is to learn a mapping from inputs (features) to outputs (labels) that can be generalized to new, unseen data. This technique is widely used in classification and regression tasks, which are pivotal in cybersecurity for identifying malware, predicting breaches, and classifying network traffic.

Applications in Cybersecurity:

- **Spam Detection**: Supervised learning can be applied to detect phishing emails and spam by training models on large datasets of labeled emails (i.e., flagged as spam or not).

■ **Intrusion Detection**: Supervised learning algorithms can identify patterns in network traffic that suggest the presence of malicious activities. Once the model is trained, it can classify incoming traffic as either benign or suspicious based on learned patterns.

Common algorithms for supervised learning include decision trees, support vector machines (SVM), and random forests, each having unique strengths for different cybersecurity scenarios.

3.1.1.2 Unsupervised Learning

Unlike supervised learning, **unsupervised learning** works with datasets that have no labeled outputs. The objective is to find hidden patterns or intrinsic structures in the data. In cybersecurity, unsupervised learning is often applied in anomaly detection, where the goal is to identify unusual behavior that may indicate a security breach or insider threat.

Applications in Cybersecurity:

■ **Anomaly Detection**: Unsupervised learning algorithms such as clustering and dimensionality reduction techniques are used to identify deviations from normal behavior in network traffic, system logs, or user activity. This is especially useful for detecting unknown or zero-day attacks.
■ **Behavioral Analytics**: Unsupervised learning can be applied to build behavioral models for users and systems, enabling the detection of deviations from established baselines that may indicate insider threats or compromised accounts.

Popular unsupervised learning algorithms include k-means clustering, hierarchical clustering, and principal component analysis (PCA).

3.1.1.3 Neural Networks and Deep Learning

Neural networks are the backbone of deep learning, a subfield of machine learning that has gained significant traction in recent years due to its ability to handle complex tasks with high accuracy. Neural networks are designed to mimic the structure and functioning of the human brain, consisting of layers of interconnected nodes (neurons) that process data and make predictions. Deep learning involves neural networks with multiple layers (deep neural networks), enabling them to learn hierarchical representations of data.

Key Concepts:

- **Layers**: Neural networks are composed of an input layer, hidden layers, and an output layer. Each layer transforms the input data in ways that enable the network to learn more abstract features.
- **Activation Functions**: These functions determine whether a neuron should be activated or not, based on the input it receives. Common activation functions include the sigmoid, tanh, and ReLU functions.
- **Backpropagation**: This is the process by which the network adjusts its weights based on the error of its predictions, allowing it to improve over time.

Applications in Cybersecurity:

- **Image and Text Recognition**: Deep learning is widely used in recognizing patterns in malware signatures, detecting phishing websites, and classifying malicious code.
- **Natural Language Processing (NLP)**: Deep learning models are used in NLP applications to detect phishing emails, malicious insider communications, and other forms of social engineering attacks by analyzing language patterns.

Neural networks and deep learning models have demonstrated their utility in complex cybersecurity tasks, especially in scenarios where large amounts of data must be processed in real time, such as in endpoint security or threat intelligence platforms.

3.2 How AI and ML Learn from Data

Data is the lifeblood of AI and ML systems. For these technologies to be effective, they must be trained on vast datasets that allow them to recognize patterns, detect anomalies, and make predictions. The process by which AI and ML learn from data involves several steps, including data collection, feature extraction, model training, and real-time analysis.

3.2.1 Training Models Using Large Datasets

AI and ML models require large datasets for training. In cybersecurity, these datasets may include logs of network traffic, records of past attacks, malware signatures, or system activity data. The goal of training is to allow the model to learn the underlying patterns or features of the data that distinguish normal activity from potential threats.

Steps in the Model Training Process:

1. **Data Collection**: The first step in training an AI or ML model is gathering relevant data. For example, in a network intrusion detection system (NIDS), data might consist of network packets captured over time.
2. **Data Preprocessing**: Once data is collected, it needs to be cleaned and preprocessed. This involves handling missing data, normalizing features, and removing outliers that could distort the training process.
3. **Feature Engineering**: Feature extraction and engineering are critical steps in preparing the data for model training. Features are the variables or attributes that the model uses to make predictions. In cybersecurity, features might include the size of a network packet, the time between connections, or the source and destination IP addresses.

3.2.2 Feature Extraction

Feature extraction is the process of transforming raw data into a set of meaningful attributes (features) that can be used by the model. Effective feature extraction is key to the success of AI and ML systems, as it enables the model to focus on the most relevant aspects of the data.

Applications in Cybersecurity:

■ **Malware Detection**: In malware detection, features might include the size of the executable, the system calls made by the program, or the network connections initiated by the malware.
■ **User Behavior Analytics**: In user behavior analytics, features might include login times, access to sensitive files, or changes in user permissions.

AI and ML models can automatically extract relevant features from large datasets, a capability that is particularly important in cybersecurity, where the volume and complexity of data can be overwhelming.

3.2.3 Real-Time Analysis

In cybersecurity, threats evolve rapidly, and the ability to perform real-time analysis is crucial. AI and ML models can process data as it is generated, allowing for immediate detection of anomalies or malicious activity. Real-time analysis is made possible through techniques such as **online learning**, where models continuously learn from new data without the need for retraining from scratch.

Examples of Real-Time Analysis in Cybersecurity:

- **Intrusion Detection Systems (IDS)**: AI-powered IDS can analyze network traffic in real time, identifying suspicious patterns that may indicate a breach.
- **Endpoint Protection**: AI and ML models running on endpoints can detect and respond to threats such as ransomware in real time, blocking attacks before they cause damage.

3.3 Case Studies of AI/ML Applications in Other Sectors

The success of AI and ML in sectors outside of cybersecurity offers valuable lessons for their application in securing digital assets. Industries such as healthcare, finance, and manufacturing have already demonstrated the transformative power of AI and ML technologies.

3.3.1 AI in Healthcare

The healthcare industry has leveraged AI and ML to revolutionize disease diagnosis, drug discovery, and patient care. AI models trained on vast amounts of medical data have proven to be highly effective in identifying patterns and correlations that are not immediately apparent to human practitioners.

Relevance to Cybersecurity:

- **Pattern Recognition**: Just as AI models can identify early signs of disease in medical imaging, similar techniques can be applied in cybersecurity to recognize the early indicators of an attack or system compromise.
- **Predictive Analytics**: Predictive models used in healthcare to forecast patient outcomes can be applied in cybersecurity to anticipate future attack vectors or emerging threats based on historical data.

3.3.2 AI in Finance

In the financial sector, AI and ML are widely used for fraud detection, risk management, and algorithmic trading. Banks and financial institutions rely on AI systems to monitor transactions in real time, detecting fraudulent activity by analyzing patterns in the data.

Relevance to Cybersecurity:

- **Fraud Detection**: The techniques used in finance to detect fraudulent transactions can be applied to detect anomalous behavior in network traffic or system activity that may indicate a cyberattack.
- **Real-Time Monitoring**: The real-time monitoring capabilities of AI systems in finance can be adapted to cybersecurity environments, where continuous monitoring of user and system behavior is essential.

3.3.3 AI in Manufacturing

Manufacturers have adopted AI and ML for predictive maintenance, quality control, and supply chain optimization. AI models analyze data from sensors embedded in machinery to predict when equipment is likely to fail, allowing for proactive maintenance.

Relevance to Cybersecurity:

- **Predictive Maintenance**: The concept of predictive maintenance can be applied in cybersecurity to anticipate system vulnerabilities or potential breaches before they occur.
- **Automation**: Just as AI-driven automation in manufacturing has improved efficiency, similar automation techniques can enhance cybersecurity protocols, enabling faster and more efficient responses to threats.

3.4 Conclusion

The foundations of AI and ML lie in their ability to learn from data, recognize patterns, and make informed decisions. By applying these principles to cybersecurity, organizations can leverage AI and ML to automate threat detection, enhance real-time analysis, and predict potential attacks with a speed and accuracy that far surpasses traditional, human-dependent methods. As illustrated, supervised learning enables the identification of known threats by learning from labeled examples of malicious and benign activity, while unsupervised learning excels at discovering novel attacks and subtle anomalies by identifying hidden patterns without prior labeling. This dual capability is critical for building a robust defense against both established and emerging cyber threats. Ultimately, the integration of AI and ML marks a paradigm shift from reactive to proactive and predictive cybersecurity. The ability of these systems to continuously learn and adapt from new data means that security postures are no longer static but can evolve in tandem with the threat landscape. However, the efficacy of these models is entirely contingent upon the quality, volume, and relevance of the data they are trained on. Therefore, for organizations to fully realize the defensive potential of AI and ML, they must first establish a foundation of robust data governance and curation processes, ensuring that the algorithms learn from a clear and comprehensive picture of their digital environment.

Chapter 4

Predictive Analytics and Threat Intelligence with AI and ML

4.1 Threat Prediction Models

One of the most promising applications of Artificial Intelligence (AI) and Machine Learning (ML) in cybersecurity is the development of threat prediction models. These models allow organizations to proactively identify potential threats and vulnerabilities before they manifest into full-scale attacks. Traditional cybersecurity strategies have been largely reactive, focusing on detection and mitigation after a breach occurs. However, the advent of AI and ML has enabled a shift toward more predictive approaches, where emerging threats can be identified, analyzed, and neutralized in advance (Figure 4.1).

In an era with unprecedented levels of cyber threats, leveraging predictive analytics in combination with threat intelligence has become essential for organizations seeking to enhance their security posture. Artificial Intelligence (AI) and Machine Learning (ML) algorithms are pivotal in analyzing vast datasets and recognizing patterns that can predict potential threats. This section explores how cybersecurity professionals can select the best threat prediction models and outlines an effective implementation process, supported by recent scholarly sources.

DOI: 10.4324/9781003615026-4

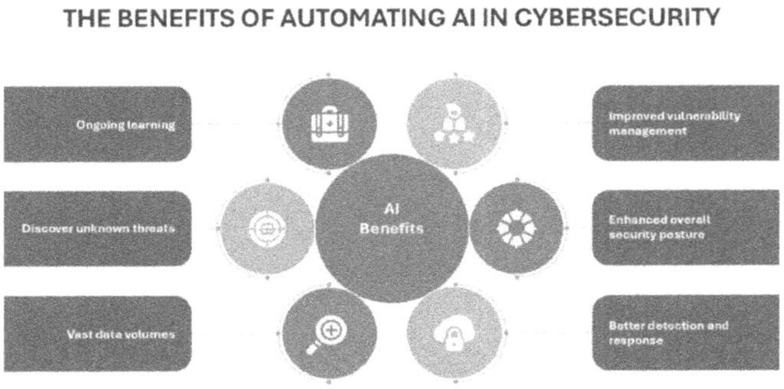

THE BENEFITS OF AUTOMATING AI IN CYBERSECURITY

Ongoing learning

Discover unknown threats

Vast data volumes

AI Benefits

Improved vulnerability management

Enhanced overall security posture

Better detection and response

Figure 4.1   The benefits of automating AI in cybersecurity

4.1.1 Selecting the Best Threat Prediction Models

Choosing the optimal threat prediction model involves several steps, which require a comprehensive understanding of the organization's objectives, data requirements, and the technical landscape within which it functions. The selection process can be effectively broken down into the following steps:

1. **Define Objectives and Requirements**: Organizations must first clarify their specific objectives regarding threat detection and prediction. Objectives may vary based on the organization's type, industry, regulatory requirements, and particular threat landscape. As highlighted by Becker et al. (2021), clear goals serve as foundational criteria for selecting appropriate models and ensuring alignment with business objectives.

2. **Assess Data Availability and Quality**: The efficacy of predictive analytics depends significantly on the quality and quantity of data available for analysis. Organizations must evaluate their existing data sources, including historical incident logs, traffic data, and user behavior metrics, to ensure they can effectively generate and consume threat intelligence, as recommended by the NIST Cybersecurity Framework (NIST, 2018). The data should be clean, structured, and comprehensive; otherwise, it may lead to inaccurate predictions. As a general principle, more diverse and extensive datasets lead to improved model performance when utilizing ML techniques.

3. **Evaluate Model Performance Metrics**: Once the objectives are clear, cybersecurity professionals should familiarize themselves with various performance metrics used to evaluate threat prediction models. Common metrics include accuracy, precision, recall, F1-score, and area under the curve (AUC). Selecting models that balance false positives

and false negatives is critical in security-sensitive environments. The practical importance of this trade-off was highlighted by Vann et al. (2020), whose research on network intrusion systems showed that an over-emphasis on minimizing false positives could lead to a dangerous increase in undetected attacks.

4. **Explore Model Options**: There are various algorithms available for predictive analytics, including supervised learning techniques, such as logistic regression, decision trees, and support vector machines, and unsupervised learning approaches like clustering algorithms. Predictive models can also harness deep learning, particularly for complex data-sets that conventional methods may struggle to analyze effectively (Xu et al., 2019). Organizations should consider conducting a comparative analysis of models through trial runs on historical data.

4.1.2 *Implementation Process of Threat Prediction Models*

After selecting suitable models, cybersecurity professionals must implement them systematically to maximize their value. The following steps outline an effective implementation process:

1. **Data Preparation and Preprocessing**: After identifying relevant datasets, professionals need to prepare them for use in selected mod-els. This preprocessing phase may involve cleaning data, normalizing inputs, addressing missing values, and transforming features to enhance model sensitivity. Data preparation is critical because the quality of the input data greatly influences the accuracy of predictions (Mala & Kottapalli, 2021).

2. **Model Training and Validation**: The next step involves splitting the prepared data into training and validation subsets. The training subset is used to teach the model to identify patterns associated with potential threats, while the validation subset is utilized to evaluate the model's performance and fine-tune parameters. As emphasized by Chikhladze et al. (2020), utilizing techniques like k-fold cross-validation can improve the reliability of model evaluations by ensuring that the model's perfor-mance is not dependent on a single data split.

3. **Deployment and Integration**: Once validated, the model can be deployed within the organization's security infrastructure. This may involve integration with existing systems, such as Security Information and Event Management (SIEM) platforms or Network Traffic Analysis (NTA) tools (Gurajala et al., 2021). Furthermore, organizations must put

in place processes for continuous monitoring to ensure the model is functioning correctly and remains effective over time.

4. **Continuous Monitoring and Improvement**: Threat landscapes evolve rapidly; thus, continuous monitoring of model performance is essential. Organizations should regularly retrain models using new datasets to adapt to emerging threats. Moreover, it is important to implement a feedback loop from security analysts. This ensures that human insights enrich predictive models and provide context that enhances their adaptability (Becker et al., 2021).

4.1.3 How Threat Prediction Models Work

Threat prediction models use historical data, network traffic logs, user behavior patterns, and other inputs to predict potential attacks. These models operate by identifying patterns and anomalies that could indicate an impending attack, using advanced statistical methods and machine learning algorithms to generate predictions.

4.1.3.1 Key Components of Threat Prediction Models

- **Training Data**: The model is trained on historical datasets, including past cyberattacks, vulnerabilities, and attack vectors. For instance, the MITRE ATT&CK framework provides a comprehensive knowledge base of known adversary tactics and techniques that can be used to train predictive models.
- **Feature Extraction**: AI/ML models extract key features from network logs, system activity, and user behaviors, such as access patterns, file modifications, and login times. These features are used to identify correlations that indicate a possible attack.
- **Anomaly Detection**: One of the central techniques in threat prediction is anomaly detection. AI/ML algorithms compare real-time data with baseline "normal" behavior to identify anomalies, which could signal an impending threat. For example, an unusual spike in outbound traffic from a particular server might indicate data exfiltration.

4.1.4 Predictive Algorithms Used in Cybersecurity

There are various machine learning algorithms that power threat prediction models, each with its unique strengths for different types of threats:

- **Decision Trees and Random Forests**: Decision trees help classify data points based on various features, while random forests enhance the accuracy by building multiple decision trees. These models are widely used for classifying malware, detecting phishing attacks, and identifying network anomalies.
- **Support Vector Machines (SVM)**: SVM is a supervised learning algorithm used for binary classification. It's particularly effective in identifying malicious traffic by classifying data as either benign or malicious.
- **Neural Networks and Deep Learning**: Deep learning models can handle complex, high-dimensional data, making them ideal for detecting sophisticated cyberattacks like advanced persistent threats (APTs) that may involve multistage exploitation techniques.

4.1.5 Threat Scenarios Predicted by AI and ML

AI and ML can predict a variety of cyber threats across different environments:

- **Malware Outbreaks**: By analyzing known malware signatures and behavioral patterns, AI systems can forecast potential malware infections, especially when combined with data on emerging threats from global threat intelligence feeds.
- **Insider Threats**: Machine learning models can predict insider threats by analyzing user behavior for deviations from established patterns, such as accessing sensitive data during unusual hours or downloading large volumes of files.
- **Distributed Denial-of-Service (DDoS) Attacks**: By analyzing traffic patterns, predictive models can forecast the likelihood of an upcoming DDoS attack based on factors like increased traffic to a specific target, unusual traffic sources, or the use of specific protocols.

4.2 Data Sources for Predictive Analytics

The effectiveness of predictive models in cybersecurity heavily depends on the quality and variety of data sources used for analysis. Big data, threat intelligence feeds, and historical breach data serve as the foundation for building accurate and reliable predictive analytics models. These datasets provide the necessary context and historical background for training AI/ML algorithms to recognize the characteristics of emerging threats.

4.2.1 Big Data in Cybersecurity

Big data in cybersecurity refers to the vast amounts of information generated by digital systems, including logs, network traffic, security alerts, and sensor data. This data is often high-velocity, high-volume, and diverse, requiring advanced analytics techniques to derive meaningful insights.

4.2.1.1 Big Data Characteristics

- **Volume**: The amount of data generated by networks, endpoints, and cloud environments is massive. AI and ML techniques are essential for analyzing this data in real time, as manual inspection would be impractical.
- **Variety**: Cybersecurity data comes in many forms, including structured logs, unstructured data such as emails, and semi-structured data like JSON objects from threat intelligence APIs.
- **Velocity**: Data must be analyzed as it is generated. The fast pace of modern cyberattacks means that delayed analysis could lead to missed threats.

4.2.1.2 Data Collection Sources

- **Network Traffic Logs**: Logs capturing inbound and outbound traffic provide crucial insights into normal network behavior and deviations that could indicate attacks.
- **System Logs**: Monitoring system processes, file modifications, and user activities helps in detecting anomalies related to malware infections or insider threats.
- **Endpoint Data**: Data collected from individual devices or endpoints, including processes, file access, and network connections, can be crucial for identifying endpoint-based attacks like ransomware.

4.2.2 Threat Intelligence Feeds

Threat intelligence feeds provide curated data on known cyber threats, including IP addresses associated with malicious activity, malware signatures, phishing URLs, and indicators of compromise (IOCs). These feeds are instrumental in training machine learning models to detect and predict new attacks based on the characteristics of past incidents.

4.2.2.1 Types of Threat Intelligence Feeds

■ **Open-Source Threat Intelligence (OSINT)**: Publicly available threat intelligence data, including sources like VirusTotal and Shodan, provides information on emerging threats and vulnerabilities.
■ **Proprietary Threat Intelligence Feeds**: Many organizations subscribe to commercial threat intelligence services like Recorded Future or FireEye, which provide detailed reports on new attack techniques, compromised credentials, and malicious actors.

4.2.2.2 Integrating Threat Intelligence

■ **Contextual Threat Analysis**: Machine learning algorithms use threat intelligence data to provide context for anomalies detected in real time. For example, if an IP address associated with a network connection appears in a threat intelligence feed, the model can prioritize it for further analysis.
■ **Proactive Defense**: AI and ML models can combine data from multiple threat intelligence sources to identify trends in cyberattacks and predict potential new vectors. For instance, if several reports indicate a rise in a particular type of ransomware, the predictive model can alert security teams to harden defenses against that threat.

4.2.3 Historical Breach Data

Historical breach data plays a critical role in training machine learning models to recognize and predict future threats. This data includes detailed information on how past cyberattacks were carried out, which vulnerabilities were exploited, and the indicators of compromise left behind.

4.2.3.1 Leveraging Historical Breach Data

■ **Attack Patterns**: AI/ML models trained on breach data can identify common attack patterns, including the stages of an attack (e.g., reconnaissance, exploitation, exfiltration), the tools used (e.g., malware variants), and the objectives (e.g., data theft, financial gain).
■ **Post-mortem Analysis**: Historical breach data can be used to conduct post-mortem analysis of past incidents, helping to refine AI/ML models to better detect similar attacks in the future.

Historical breach data allows AI/ML models to learn from the mistakes of the past, ensuring that organizations are better prepared to predict and respond to emerging threats.

4.3 Real-Time Threat Monitoring and Analysis

Real-time threat monitoring and analysis is a critical component of modern cybersecurity, enabling organizations to detect and respond to threats as they occur. AI and ML technologies enhance real-time monitoring capabilities by automating the detection of anomalies, correlating data from multiple sources, and prioritizing security alerts for investigation. This section explores how AI/ML algorithms power continuous threat monitoring and analysis.

4.3.1 AI/ML Algorithms for Real-Time Monitoring

Real-time monitoring requires high-performance algorithms capable of processing large volumes of data with low latency. The following AI/ML techniques are commonly used to support real-time threat detection:

- **Streaming Data Analysis**: AI/ML models are designed to analyze data streams in real time, identifying patterns of malicious activity as they unfold. This capability is critical for detecting fast-moving attacks like ransomware or data exfiltration.
- **Reinforcement Learning**: Reinforcement learning algorithms learn and adapt over time by interacting with the environment. In cybersecurity, these models can autonomously update their detection rules as they observe new attack techniques in real time.
- Event Correlation: AI algorithms can correlate events from different sources, such as network logs, user activities, and system alerts, to identify the relationships between seemingly unrelated incidents. This correlation helps detect complex, multistage attacks that would otherwise go unnoticed.

4.3.2 Network Traffic Monitoring

AI-driven network traffic monitoring enables organizations to detect anomalies in data flow across the network. Machine learning models continuously analyze packets, looking for patterns that indicate potential threats, such as unexpected traffic spikes, unusual ports, or connections to known malicious domains.

4.3.2.1 Applications in Network Security

- **DDoS Detection**: AI models can monitor incoming traffic and detect signs of a Distributed Denial-of-Service (DDoS) attack, such as traffic flooding from multiple IP addresses.
- **Packet Inspection**: Deep packet inspection (DPI) techniques, enhanced with AI, allow for real-time analysis of network packets to identify malware signatures or suspicious payloads.

4.3.3 Endpoint Threat Detection

Endpoints are often the weakest link in cybersecurity defenses, making them prime targets for attackers. AI-powered endpoint threat detection tools analyze data collected from devices, including application usage, file access, and system processes, to detect anomalies that may indicate compromise.

4.3.3.1 Real-Time Endpoint Monitoring

- **Behavioral Analytics**: Machine learning models build behavioral profiles for each endpoint, flagging deviations from normal.

In conclusion, predictive analytics powered by AI and ML is crucial for enhancing threat intelligence in cybersecurity. By carefully selecting the best threat prediction models and following a structured implementation process, cybersecurity professionals can empower their organizations to detect threats proactively and respond effectively. Faced with increasingly sophisticated threats, the importance of integrating these predictive capabilities into security frameworks cannot be overstated.

Chapter 5

Automating Security Protocols Using AI and ML

5.1 Automation in Cybersecurity: How AI and ML Are Enabling Automated Response Systems

Cybersecurity is facing an unprecedented wave of challenges due to increasing attack complexity, volume, and speed. Human-centered defense strategies are increasingly outpaced by attackers leveraging automation and advanced tools. The integration of Artificial Intelligence (AI) and Machine Learning (ML) has revolutionized the cybersecurity landscape, especially by enabling automation in security protocols. This transformation allows organizations to stay ahead of cybercriminals by automating threat detection, response, and mitigation processes, thus ensuring timely and effective defense mechanisms (Figure 5.1).

BENEFITS OF USING AI IN CYBERSECURITY

Figure 5.1   Benefits of using AI in cybersecurity

    DOI: 10.4324/9781003615026-5

As cyber threats continue to evolve in complexity and frequency, organizations must adopt innovative strategies to enhance their cybersecurity posture. One such strategy is the automation of cybersecurity protocols through the use of Artificial Intelligence (AI) and Machine Learning (ML). Automation not only streamlines security processes but also enables faster, more effective responses to threats, thus empowering organizations to safeguard their assets more efficiently.

5.1.1 Improving the Organizational Security Posture

Automating cybersecurity protocols significantly enhances an organization's security posture by reducing the burden on security teams and minimizing human error. According to a study by Bansal et al. (2021), the use of automation in Security Operations Centers (SOCs) can lead to improved incident response times by up to 80% as repetitive, time-consuming tasks are handled by automated systems rather than relying solely on manual interventions.

By automating routine security processes—such as log analysis, patch management, and vulnerability assessments—organizations can focus their resources on higher-level security tasks, such as strategy development and threat hunting. This delegation of tasks to automated systems allows for continuous monitoring of systems and networks, enabling the swift identification of anomalies that might indicate a security breach (Xia et al., 2022).

Additionally, AI and ML can analyze large volumes of data in real time, allowing organizations to identify patterns that are indicative of potential threats or vulnerabilities. This heightened level of observability significantly improves the ability to assess security risk and proactively implement measures to mitigate identified issues. Research conducted by Papadopoulos et al. (2020) highlights how employing automated solutions for threat detection leads to not only quicker identification of security breaches but also a reduction in the average cost of a data breach, enhancing the overall operational resilience of organizations.

5.1.2 Enabling Automated Response Systems

AI and ML play a crucial role in enabling automated response systems within cybersecurity frameworks. Automated response systems utilize predefined rules and algorithms to react to identified threats without requiring human intervention. For instance, when an anomaly is detected, an automated response system can isolate affected systems, block suspicious traffic, and initiate incident response protocols in real time (McAfee, 2020).

According to a case study by Kaur et al. (2021), deploying AI-enhanced Security Orchestration, Automation, and Response (SOAR) tools allows organizations to standardize and automate incident response workflows. Such tools can automatically gather contextual information related to the threat, assess current vulnerabilities, and recommend or enact appropriate remediation actions. The integration of AI into these systems not only supports faster containment of threats but also reduces the incident backlog often faced by security teams, ensuring that human analysts can focus on complex, higher-priority issues.

In addition, the combination of AI and ML in incident response can improve the accuracy of threat prioritization. By analyzing historical data and previous incident responses, ML algorithms can learn to classify threats by severity to improve resource allocation. The practical viability of this approach was confirmed by Rehman et al. (2021), whose case study showed that an ML-powered prioritization system helped a financial institution reduce false positives by 60% while ensuring all critical threats were addressed.

5.1.3 Staying Ahead of Cyber Criminals

Automation, driven by AI and ML, allows organizations to stay ahead of cyber criminals by continually adapting to the shifting threat landscape. Criminals are increasingly employing sophisticated techniques and technology, and organizations must match their pace of innovation to prevent successful attacks.

Automated security systems can consistently update themselves with the latest threat intelligence feeds, leveraging data from multiple sources to enhance their understanding of current threat vectors. This capability enables organizations to immediately adapt their defenses based on emerging threats, effectively reducing the chances of a successful attack (Alazab et al., 2020).

Furthermore, automation allows organizations to proactively conduct security assessments, such as penetration testing and phishing simulations, on a scheduled basis without straining resources. The primary benefit of automation is the ability to conduct proactive security assessments continuously. Research by Rauscher et al. (2021) provided empirical support for this, showing that organizations using automated penetration testing tools fixed critical vulnerabilities an average of 45 days faster than those relying on manual tests. This proactive security posture inherently makes it more challenging for criminals to find exploitable entry points (Figure 5.2).

6 WAYS TO IMPROVE CYBERSECURITY WITH AI AND ML

Figure 5.2 Six ways to improve cybersecurity with AI and ML

5.1.4 The Case for Automation in Cybersecurity

Traditional cybersecurity strategies have often relied on manual processes, with analysts reviewing logs, monitoring alerts, and reacting to breaches after they occur. This reactive approach has led to several challenges, including:

- **Alert Fatigue**: Security Operations Center (SOC) teams are frequently overwhelmed by the sheer volume of alerts, many of which turn out to be false positives.
- **Slow Response Times**: Delayed responses to emerging threats can lead to significant damage before mitigation steps are initiated.
- **Human Error**: Manual processes are prone to human error, leading to missed threats or incorrect responses.

By integrating AI and ML, security systems can autonomously detect and mitigate threats, significantly reducing the need for human intervention. This automation enables organizations to respond more quickly and effectively, minimizing damage and enhancing security postures.

5.1.5 Types of Security Automations Enabled by AI/ML

AI and ML technologies offer several automation capabilities across various cybersecurity functions, such as:

- **Threat Detection**: AI/ML models continuously monitor networks and systems for abnormal behavior, identifying threats in real time.
- **Incident Response**: Automated response systems, powered by AI, initiate pre-programmed responses to specific threats, such as isolating infected devices or blocking malicious traffic.

- **Vulnerability Management**: AI-driven systems automatically scan for known vulnerabilities in software and hardware, suggesting or implementing patches where necessary.
- **Phishing Detection**: Automated phishing detection tools use ML algorithms to analyze emails, recognizing signs of phishing attempts and preventing them from reaching users.

5.1.6 The Shift toward Security Orchestration, Automation, and Response (SOAR)

Security Orchestration, Automation, and Response (SOAR) platforms have emerged as a key technology enabling automated security operations. SOAR integrates AI-driven analytics and ML algorithms to automate incident detection and response, while orchestrating the flow of information across various security tools.

- **Orchestration**: SOAR systems manage data from multiple sources (e.g., intrusion detection systems, endpoint protection, threat intelligence platforms) to create a cohesive security landscape.
- **Automation**: The platforms automate repetitive security tasks, such as alert triage, threat analysis, and the execution of playbooks designed to counter specific types of attacks.
- **Response**: SOAR platforms use AI to respond automatically to threats, such as blocking malicious IPs, quarantining compromised devices, or generating detailed reports for further analysis.

SOAR platforms are increasingly adopted across industries for their ability to reduce the time between detection and response, streamline workflows, and enhance overall security.

5.2 Automated Incident Detection and Response: Tools and Technologies That Use AI/ML to Identify and Respond to Security Incidents with Minimal Human Intervention

Incident detection and response have traditionally required the constant monitoring of security environments by human analysts. However, given the speed and sophistication of modern cyberattacks, AI and ML technologies are being leveraged to enable rapid and, in some cases, fully automated incident detection and response mechanisms.

5.2.1 Incident Detection Using AI/ML

AI/ML algorithms have proven highly effective in incident detection, particularly through their capacity to analyze vast amounts of data in real time and identify anomalies that indicate security breaches. These algorithms detect subtle patterns in behavior that are indicative of attacks, such as unusual login locations, sudden data transfers, or anomalies in network traffic.

5.2.1.1 Techniques Used in Incident Detection

- **Anomaly Detection**: ML models are trained to recognize normal behavior within an environment. When the system detects deviations from this behavior, it flags the activity as potentially malicious. For instance, a sudden spike in file access attempts may indicate an insider threat or a data exfiltration attempt.
- **Signature-based Detection**: While anomaly detection identifies new or unknown threats, signature-based detection uses predefined patterns of known threats (such as malware signatures) to quickly identify and isolate malicious activities.
- **Behavioral Analytics**: Advanced systems continuously track the behavior of users, devices, and systems, flagging unusual or suspicious activities, such as an employee accessing sensitive files they do not normally interact with.

5.2.2 Automated Incident Response Systems

In addition to detecting incidents, AI/ML technologies also facilitate automated response mechanisms that can be triggered with minimal human intervention. These systems reduce response times and enable swift countermeasures to be implemented once a threat is detected.

5.2.2.1 Key Components of Automated Incident Response

- **Predefined Playbooks**: Automated response systems operate based on predefined playbooks, which outline the steps to be taken when specific threats are detected. For example, in the event of a malware infection, the playbook may isolate the infected system from the network, delete malicious files, and initiate a scan across all endpoints.

- **Adaptive Learning**: Machine learning enables response systems to adapt to new and evolving threats. As the system encounters new types of attacks, it refines its responses, making future mitigations more effective.
- **Self-healing Systems**: Some AI/ML-powered security systems are designed to be self-healing. When an attack compromises a part of the system, the automated response may include rolling back compromised files, restoring previous system configurations, and ensuring continued system availability.

5.2.2.2 Example Technologies

- **Endpoint Detection and Response (EDR)**: EDR systems are equipped with AI/ML capabilities that provide real-time monitoring and automated responses to endpoint threats, such as ransomware or zero-day exploits.
- **Intrusion Detection Systems (IDS) and Intrusion Prevention Systems (IPS)**: AI-enhanced IDS/IPS technologies monitor network traffic and system activities to identify intrusions. Upon detecting an intrusion, the system can either alert administrators or automatically initiate mitigation processes, such as blocking malicious traffic.
- **AI-Driven Security Information and Event Management (SIEM)**: Modern SIEM platforms leverage AI and ML to correlate security events from various sources, filter out false positives, and trigger automated responses to high-confidence threats.

5.2.3 *Limitations of Automated Incident Detection and Response*

Despite the significant advantages of automated incident detection and response, there are some limitations that organizations must consider:

- **False Positives**: AI/ML models may still generate false positives, especially during the early stages of implementation. These false positives may overwhelm the response system or require manual intervention to distinguish genuine threats from benign anomalies.
- **Attack Sophistication**: While automation can handle many routine security tasks, highly sophisticated, multistage attacks may still require human oversight and manual intervention.

■ **Data Privacy and Compliance**: Automated systems must adhere to data privacy regulations (e.g., GDPR, CCPA), especially when handling personal data. Ensuring that automated responses do not violate these regulations is essential.

5.3 Adaptive Security Systems: Systems That Adjust to New Threats Based on Real-Time Data and Predictive Analysis

AI and ML technologies have ushered in the era of adaptive security systems that dynamically adjust their defense mechanisms based on real-time data and predictive analysis. These systems go beyond predefined rules and static policies, continuously learning from the evolving threat landscape to enhance their response capabilities.

5.3.1 What Is Adaptive Security?

Adaptive security refers to the ability of a security system to modify its behavior based on changes in the environment, such as new attack vectors, emerging malware strains, or shifts in user behavior. Unlike traditional security models, which rely on fixed rules and signatures, adaptive systems are fluid and flexible, capable of responding to both known and unknown threats.

5.3.1.1 Characteristics of Adaptive Security Systems

■ **Context-Aware**: Adaptive systems consider the broader context of an event, such as the user's typical behavior, the time of day, or the geographic location, before deciding whether an action is suspicious or malicious.
■ **Self-Learning**: Adaptive security systems use machine learning to continuously update their understanding of what constitutes normal and abnormal activity. As new data is fed into the system, it refines its models to improve future predictions.
■ **Dynamic Policies**: Adaptive systems do not rely on static rules. Instead, they adjust security policies dynamically, responding to evolving threats without requiring manual rule updates.

5.3.2 Real-Time Data and Predictive Analysis in Adaptive Security

The backbone of adaptive security systems is their ability to leverage real-time data and predictive analytics to anticipate and mitigate threats. These systems are built on the following components:

5.3.2.1 Real-Time Data Processing

- **Continuous Monitoring**: Adaptive systems continuously collect data from various sources, such as network traffic, endpoint activity, and cloud environments. This real-time data provides insights into current operations and potential threats.
- **Automated Data Correlation**: By correlating data from multiple sources, adaptive systems gain a holistic view of the threat landscape. For instance, an increase in traffic to a sensitive database combined with unusual user behavior may indicate a potential data breach.
- **Real-time Adjustments**: As the system detects new threats or changes in network behavior, it can make real-time adjustments, such as tightening access controls or deploying additional security measures.

5.3.2.2 Predictive Analysis

- **Predicting Future Threats**: Adaptive systems use predictive analytics to forecast potential threats based on historical data, threat intelligence, and emerging trends. For example, if a specific malware variant is spreading globally, the system can proactively adjust defenses to mitigate the threat before it impacts the organization.
- **Proactive Threat Hunting**: Predictive models enable security teams to engage in proactive threat hunting, identifying vulnerabilities and weaknesses before they can be exploited by attackers.

5.3.3 The Role of AI/ML in Building Adaptive Security Systems

AI and ML play a critical role in adaptive security by enabling systems to learn from experience, predict threats, and respond autonomously. Key contributions of AI/ML include:

5.3.3.1 AI-Enhanced Threat Intelligence

■ **AI-driven Threat Intelligence Platforms (TIPs)**: These platforms aggregate data from various sources, including global threat feeds, historical attack data, and security alerts. By leveraging AI algorithms, TIPs identify new threats and adjust security postures accordingly.

5.3.3.2 ML-Based Anomaly Detection

■ **Enhanced Behavioral Analytics**: Machine learning models track user and entity behavior, identifying anomalies that deviate from established norms. These systems evolve over time, becoming more accurate in distinguishing between benign and malicious activities.

5.3.3.3 Predictive ML Models

■ **Threat Predictions**: By analyzing past attacks and current threat trends, ML models predict potential future attacks. These predictions enable adaptive systems to take preemptive measures, reducing the impact of new or emerging threats.

5.4 Conclusion

The adoption of AI and ML technologies is reshaping the cybersecurity landscape, especially in automating security protocols and enabling adaptive defense mechanisms. By enhancing the efficiency and effectiveness of security operations, enabling rapid response systems, and supporting continuous adaptation to emerging threats, organizations can significantly mitigate risks and stay several steps ahead of cyber criminals. Automation in cybersecurity not only accelerates incident detection and response but also enhances the overall effectiveness of security measures. Adaptive systems represent the future of cybersecurity, where real-time data and predictive analysis work hand in hand to proactively mitigate threats. As AI and ML technologies continue to evolve, their ability to anticipate, detect, and respond to threats will become an essential component of modern cybersecurity strategies.

Chapter 6

AI-Powered Intrusion Detection and Prevention Systems (IDPS)

As the complexity and sophistication of cyber threats have increased over the past decade, so too has the need for more advanced security measures. Intrusion Detection and Prevention Systems (IDPS) have long been a cornerstone of cybersecurity strategies, tasked with identifying and preventing malicious activities. While traditional IDPS has been effective to a certain degree, the emergence of Artificial Intelligence (AI) and Machine Learning (ML) has significantly enhanced their capabilities. AI-powered IDPS can analyze vast amounts of data, recognize patterns, detect anomalies, and respond to potential threats in real time.

As the digital landscape evolves, the complexity and sophistication of cyber threats have escalated significantly. In response to these evolving threats, organizations are increasingly turning to advanced security measures, such as AI-Powered Intrusion Detection and Prevention Systems (IDPS). These systems leverage machine learning (ML) and artificial intelligence (AI) to provide more effective threat detection, real-time response capabilities, and enhanced overall cybersecurity protocols.

6.1 The Need for Advanced Security Measures

The proliferation of sophisticated cyber threats has necessitated a paradigm shift in how organizations approach cybersecurity. Traditional security

DOI: 10.4324/9781003615026-6

measures, which primarily relied on signature-based detection methods, are increasingly inadequate against modern threats that utilize advanced evasion techniques. According to a report by the Cybersecurity and Infrastructure Security Agency (CISA), cyber threats, including ransomware, advanced persistent threats (APTs), and zero-day vulnerabilities, have surged, with healthcare, finance, and critical infrastructure sectors being particularly targeted (CISA, 2021).

The dynamic nature of cyberattacks—characterized by rapid mutation and the use of polymorphic malware—demands that organizations adopt proactive and adaptive security solutions. Traditional IDPS systems, which often rely on static rules or hard-coded signatures to identify threats, may overlook advanced or previously unknown attacks, leading to significant security gaps (He et al., 2020). The increasing frequency and sophistication of cyber intrusions have prompted security professionals to seek solutions that can adapt and learn from evolving attack patterns to protect sensitive data and systems more effectively.

6.2 Enhancing Cybersecurity Protocols with AI and ML

AI and ML offer promising avenues for enhancing traditional security measures by improving the accuracy of threat detection and response capabilities. By incorporating AI into IDPS, organizations can significantly augment their cybersecurity posture.

1. **Anomaly Detection**: AI algorithms employ various statistical models and neural networks to analyze vast amounts of network traffic data and user behavior. By establishing a baseline of what constitutes normal behavior, these systems can identify anomalies that deviate from typical patterns, which may indicate potential intrusions (Bertino & Islam, 2019). The superiority of AI-driven IDPS in detecting unknown threats is supported by research, including a 2021 study by Kwon et al., which demonstrated their effectiveness leading to earlier breach detection.
2. **Predictive Analytics**: AI-powered IDPS also integrates predictive analytics, allowing organizations to foresee potential threats before they materialize. Machine learning models can analyze historical data and trending patterns to identify vulnerabilities and probable points of attack. The logic of a proactive approach is that it allows countermeasures to be implemented before an attack occurs. The practical

effectiveness of this strategy was confirmed by Li et al. (2020), whose simulation showed that proactive patching based on threat intelligence was twice as effective as reactive patching at preventing intrusions.

3. **Real-Time Adaptation**: Unlike traditional systems, AI and ML-based IDPS can adapt in real time to new threats. These systems can continuously learn from new data inputs and adjust their detection algorithms accordingly, ensuring that the IDPS remains effective even against previously unencountered threats. This continual evolution is imperative because cybercriminals continuously refine their tactics to evade detection (Suresh & Akthar, 2021).

4. **Reduced False Positives**: One of the challenges facing traditional IDPS has been the high rate of false positives, which can overwhelm security teams and lead to alert fatigue. AI and ML-powered systems utilize advanced classification methods to filter out benign alerts effectively, allowing security teams to focus on genuine threats. Research by Mohammed, Nataraj, Chikkagoudar, Chandrasekaran, and Manjunath (2021) indicates that AI-based detection methods significantly reduce false positive rates while maintaining high detection accuracy, enabling security personnel to allocate their resources more effectively.

5. **Enhanced Incident Response**: The integration of AI also facilitates improved incident response capabilities. By analyzing real-time threats and correlating them with historical incidents, AI systems can provide actionable insights and recommend appropriate response actions. This capability enables quicker containment and remediation of breaches, minimizing potential damage (Siddiqui et al., 2021).

In summary, as cyber threats grow more complex and sophisticated, the necessity for advanced security measures becomes paramount. AI-Powered Intrusion Detection and Prevention Systems offer organizations a means to enhance traditional cybersecurity protocols effectively. By employing AI and ML, organizations can improve anomaly detection, predictive analytics, real-time adaptation, reduction of false positives, and incident response capabilities, thereby fortifying their defenses against evolving cyber threats. This chapter explores the transformative impact of AI on IDPS, comparing traditional systems with AI-driven ones, examining key AI/ML algorithms used in intrusion detection, and analyzing case studies that demonstrate the effectiveness of AI-powered IDPS across various industries.

6.3 Traditional vs. AI-Powered IDPS: Key Differences in Effectiveness and Efficiency

6.3.1 Traditional Intrusion Detection and Prevention Systems (IDPS)

Traditional IDPS relies heavily on predefined rules, signatures, and heuristic methods to detect and prevent intrusions. These systems are designed to monitor network traffic, detect suspicious activities, and respond to known attack patterns. Two key types of traditional IDPS are:

- **Signature-based IDPS**: These systems compare network traffic against a database of known attack signatures. When a match is found, an alert is triggered. However, signature-based systems are only effective against known threats and often struggle to detect new, evolving attack vectors such as zero-day exploits.
- **Anomaly-based IDPS**: Anomaly-based systems establish a baseline for normal network behavior. Any deviations from this baseline are flagged as potential threats. While anomaly-based systems can detect previously unknown attacks, they tend to produce high rates of false positives, requiring manual intervention and fine-tuning.

The limitations of traditional IDPS are becoming increasingly evident as cyberattacks become more complex, dynamic, and automated. These systems often fail to detect sophisticated threats such as advanced persistent threats (APTs), polymorphic malware, and coordinated attacks that evolve over time. Additionally, traditional IDPS lacks the ability to learn from past events and improve its detection capabilities without manual updates.

6.3.2 AI-Powered Intrusion Detection and Prevention Systems (IDPS)

AI-powered IDPS represents a significant leap forward in the field of cyber-security. By integrating AI and ML algorithms, these systems can analyze massive amounts of data, identify subtle patterns, and adapt to new threats without requiring manual intervention. Key advantages of AI-powered IDPS include:

■ **Real-Time Threat Detection**: AI-powered systems can process large datasets in real time, enabling faster detection and response to emerging threats.

■ **Anomaly Detection with Lower False Positives**: Unlike traditional anomaly-based systems, AI-powered IDPS can distinguish between benign and malicious anomalies more accurately, significantly reducing the number of false positives.

■ **Adaptive Learning**: AI-powered IDPS can learn from historical data and continuously improve its detection models, making them more effective at identifying both known and unknown threats.

■ **Scalability**: AI systems can scale to monitor large, complex networks across multiple environments, such as cloud infrastructure, mobile devices, and Internet of Things (IoT) networks.

6.4 AI/ML Algorithms in Intrusion Detection: How Algorithms like Anomaly Detection and Clustering Are Being Used to Identify Intrusions

The power of AI in IDPS comes from the sophisticated algorithms that drive its ability to detect intrusions with greater precision and efficiency. Several AI and ML algorithms have proven particularly effective in the realm of intrusion detection and prevention. The most widely used techniques include anomaly detection, clustering, decision trees, and neural networks.

6.4.1 Anomaly Detection

Anomaly detection is a key technique in AI-powered IDPS. It works by identifying deviations from the norm, which can signal potential intrusions. AI systems are particularly adept at anomaly detection due to their ability to model complex and non-linear patterns. There are three primary types of anomaly detection algorithms:

■ **Supervised Learning**: In supervised learning, the model is trained using labeled data, where normal and abnormal behaviors are clearly defined. Once trained, the system can classify new data as normal or anomalous. Supervised learning is highly effective in detecting known types of attacks but may struggle with novel threats.

- **Unsupervised Learning**: Unsupervised learning models work without labeled data, instead learning to identify normal behavior patterns on their own. Any data that deviates from these patterns is flagged as anomalous. Unsupervised learning is valuable for detecting new, previously unknown threats but may require more fine-tuning to reduce false positives.
- **Semi-supervised Learning**: This hybrid approach uses a combination of labeled and unlabeled data to improve anomaly detection. Semi-supervised learning can be particularly useful when labeled data are scarce or expensive to obtain.

6.4.2 Clustering

Clustering algorithms group data points based on their similarity to one another. In the context of IDPS, clustering is used to identify groups of similar network activities or user behaviors. If a cluster contains activities that are significantly different from the norm, it is flagged for further investigation. Common clustering algorithms include:

- **K-Means Clustering**: This algorithm divides data into K clusters based on the distance between data points and the cluster centers. It is particularly useful for identifying groups of related malicious activities.
- **Hierarchical Clustering**: Hierarchical clustering builds a tree-like structure of clusters, where each level represents different degrees of similarity. This technique is useful for detecting multistage attacks that evolve over time.
- **DBSCAN (Density-Based Spatial Clustering of Applications with Noise)**: DBSCAN identifies clusters based on the density of data points, which is useful for detecting outliers and sparse patterns, often characteristic of intrusions.

6.4.3 Neural Networks and Deep Learning

Neural networks, especially deep learning models, have emerged as powerful tools for intrusion detection. Deep learning models can automatically extract features from raw data, making them particularly effective at detecting complex attack patterns and previously unknown threats. Common neural network architectures used in IDPS include:

- **Convolutional Neural Networks (CNNs)**: While primarily used in image processing, CNNs can also be applied to cybersecurity by detecting spatial patterns in network traffic data.
- **Recurrent Neural Networks (RNNs)**: RNNs are particularly useful for analyzing sequential data, such as time-series logs or network traffic patterns. RNNs can detect temporal dependencies between events, making them well-suited for identifying APTs or multistage attacks.

6.5 Case Studies of AI-Powered IDPS: Real-World Examples and Results from Financial, Healthcare, and Government Sectors

AI-powered IDPS has already been deployed in a variety of industries, delivering significant improvements in both threat detection and response. The following case studies highlight the effectiveness of AI-powered IDPS in real-world applications across the financial, healthcare, and government sectors.

6.5.1 Financial Sector: AI-Powered IDPS in Banking

Banks and financial institutions are frequent targets for cybercriminals due to the highly sensitive nature of the data they handle. AI-powered IDPS has become an essential tool for securing financial networks against increasingly sophisticated attacks. In one notable case, a large multinational bank deployed an AI-powered IDPS to monitor its global network of ATMs, branches, and online services.

- **The Challenge**: The bank was struggling to keep up with the increasing volume of cyberattacks, including phishing, ransomware, and Distributed Denial-of-Service (DDoS) attacks. Traditional IDPS was generating too many false positives, overwhelming the security team and delaying responses to actual threats.
- **The Solution**: By implementing an AI-powered IDPS, the bank was able to significantly reduce the number of false positives while improving detection rates for zero-day exploits and insider threats. The AI system continuously learned from new data, adapting its models to evolving threats in real time.

- **Results**: The bank reported a 40% reduction in the number of successful attacks and a 60% decrease in the time it took to respond to incidents. Additionally, the system flagged several previously undetected insider threats, which were mitigated before any data loss occurred.

6.5.2 Healthcare Sector: Protecting Patient Data with AI-Powered IDPS

The healthcare industry faces unique cybersecurity challenges, particularly due to the sensitive nature of patient data and the increasing reliance on connected medical devices. In one case, a major hospital system implemented AI-powered IDPS to protect its networks from ransomware and other threats.

- **The Challenge**: The hospital had experienced several ransomware attacks, leading to the encryption of patient records and significant disruptions to healthcare services. Traditional IDPS was unable to detect the ransomware in time, allowing the attackers to encrypt critical systems before any response was initiated.
- **The Solution**: The hospital deployed an AI-powered IDPS to monitor its network for early signs of ransomware and other malware. The AI system was trained on historical data, allowing it to detect unusual file access patterns, rapid encryption activities, and anomalous network traffic.
- **Results**: Within six months of deployment, the hospital experienced a dramatic reduction in ransomware incidents. The AI system was able to detect and block several ransomware attempts in their early stages, preventing any data loss. Additionally, the system helped identify vulnerabilities in medical devices connected to the network, which were subsequently patched.

6.5.3 Government Sector: Securing National Infrastructure with AI-Powered IDPS

Government agencies, particularly those responsible for critical infrastructure, are prime targets for cyberattacks. In an era marked by increasingly sophisticated cyber threats, government agencies face the dual challenge of protecting sensitive information and maintaining the integrity of critical national infrastructure. As the primary custodians of national security and public resources, government entities must elevate their security protocols to effectively counteract the relentless wave of cyberattacks targeting vital services such as energy grids, water supply systems, and emergency response networks. One promising solution is the deployment of AI-Powered Intrusion Detection and Prevention Systems (IDPS), which can enhance situational awareness and bolster defenses against cyber threats.

6.5.3.1 The Need for Improved Security Protocols in Government Agencies

Government agencies represent prime targets for sophisticated cybercriminals and state-sponsored actors due to the sensitive and valuable information they manage. Recent studies highlight that cyberattacks against government institutions have increased exponentially in recent years, driven by geopolitical tensions and the increasing availability of sophisticated hacking tools (Fung et al., 2021). For instance, high-profile incidents like the SolarWinds cyberattack illustrate how adversaries exploit vulnerabilities to infiltrate government networks and exfiltrate sensitive data, raising concerns about national security and citizen safety (CISA, 2021).

Moreover, government agencies often grapple with legacy systems that may not be equipped to handle modern threats, rendering their cybersecurity frameworks inadequate. According to the US Government Accountability Office (Gamble, 2020), many federal agencies lack robust security protocols and struggle with outdated infrastructure, which can lead to significant vulnerabilities and limited responsiveness to emerging threats. As cyber adversaries increasingly employ advanced persistent threats (APTs) and sophisticated techniques, government entities must reassess and enhance their security postures to safeguard sensitive data and essential public services.

6.5.3.2 The Role of AI-Powered IDPS in Protecting Critical Infrastructure

Given the critical role that government agencies play in safeguarding national infrastructure, adopting AI-powered IDPS can be paramount in fortifying defenses against cyber threats. Critical infrastructure sectors, such as energy and water supply systems, are particularly vulnerable to cyberattacks that could disrupt services, cause financial losses, and even endanger lives. AI-enhanced IDPS can significantly bolster the security of these vital services.

1. **Enhanced Threat Detection**: AI-powered IDPS utilizes machine learning algorithms to analyze real-time data streams from various sources, including sensors and network traffic, to identify anomalous behavior that may signify a cyberattack. Research conducted by Khraisat et al. (2020) shows that AI and ML techniques can detect unknown threats more effectively than traditional systems by leveraging vast amounts of historical data to create a baseline of normal operation. This capability is critical for infrastructure operators, allowing them to detect potential intrusions before they escalate into serious incidents.

2. **Proactive Threat Mitigation**: Proactive threat mitigation is vital in sectors like energy and water supply, where downtime or disruptions can have severe consequences. AI-powered IDPS solutions can implement automatic responses to detected threats, allowing for real-time containment and remediation of incidents. Automated systems are crucial for critical infrastructure protection. For example, upon detecting unusual activity indicative of a cyberattack targeting an energy grid, a system could automatically isolate affected components. This capability for rapid response is essential for maintaining operational integrity, a point supported by research into resilient infrastructure (Raghavan et al., 2021).

3. **Comprehensive Security Posture**: Given the interconnected nature of critical infrastructure systems, it is vital that government agencies deploy cybersecurity measures that encompass all components of their operational environments. AI-driven IDPS can provide a holistic view of the threat landscape, integrating data from various infrastructure elements, thereby improving situational awareness and enabling informed decision-making. A comprehensive approach ensures that all aspects of national infrastructure are protected against coordinated cyber threats (Stouffer et al., 2017).

4. **Regulatory Compliance and Risk Management**: Governments are often held to strict regulatory standards and guidelines. Implementing AI-powered IDPS can help ensure that agencies remain compliant with security frameworks, such as the National Institute of Standards and Technology (NIST) Cybersecurity Framework. By integrating AI into their security measures, agencies can facilitate continuous monitoring, implement risk assessments, and maintain logs and audit trails essential for meeting compliance requirements (Alcaraz et al., 2021).

In one case, a national government deployed an AI-powered IDPS to protect its energy grid and water supply systems from cyber threats.

- **The Challenge**: The government was facing a growing number of cyberattacks aimed at disrupting national infrastructure. These attacks included DDoS attacks, APTs, and attempts to compromise industrial control systems (ICS). Traditional IDPS struggled to detect these highly coordinated, multistage attacks.
- **The Solution**: By implementing an AI-powered IDPS, the government was able to monitor its entire network of critical infrastructure in real time. The AI system used advanced anomaly detection and clustering algorithms to identify coordinated attacks across multiple locations.
- **Results**: The government successfully thwarted several major cyberattacks, including attempts to shut down power plants and water treatment facilities. The AI-powered IDPS allowed security teams to identify and neutralize threats before any damage was done, enhancing the overall resilience of the nation's critical infrastructure.

6.6 Conclusion

The integration of AI and ML into Intrusion Detection and Prevention Systems has revolutionized the way organizations detect and respond to cyber threats. AI-powered IDPS offers significant advantages over traditional systems, including enhanced detection capabilities, reduced false positives, and the ability to adapt to evolving threats in real time. As the cybersecurity landscape continues to evolve, the role of AI in protecting critical infrastructure, sensitive data, and financial assets will only become more important. By leveraging the power of AI and ML, organizations can stay ahead of cybercriminals and ensure the security of their networks. Government agencies are uniquely positioned to enhance their security protocols in response to the ever-looming threats posed by sophisticated cyber adversaries. By deploying AI-powered IDPS to protect critical infrastructure, such as energy grids and water supply systems, agencies can significantly improve their ability to detect, respond to, and mitigate cyber threats effectively. Adopting such advanced security measures will not only fortify the integrity of national infrastructure but also ensure the safety and security of citizens in an increasingly digital world.

Chapter 7

AI and ML in Endpoint Security and Zero Trust Models

As cyber threats continue to evolve in complexity and frequency, the imperative for advanced security frameworks has never been more critical. The rise of sophisticated techniques, such as ransomware, advanced persistent threats (APTs), and exploitation of zero-day vulnerabilities, emphasizes the urgent need for organizations to adapt their security postures accordingly. Traditional security measures, which often focus on perimeter defense and reactive strategies, are increasingly inadequate in protecting against dynamic threats that target endpoints directly.

7.1 The Critical Need for Advanced Security Frameworks

The changing landscape of cyber threats has highlighted several vulnerabilities within traditional cybersecurity frameworks. For example, research from Cybersecurity Ventures projects that cybercrime will cost the global economy $10.5 trillion annually by 2025, indicating a massive increase in the financial implications of inadequate security measures (Morgan, 2020). Notably, endpoint devices—such as laptops, smartphones, and IoT devices—are now common attack vectors for cyber adversaries, making endpoint security an essential component of a comprehensive cybersecurity strategy (Figure 7.1).

RISK MANAGEMENT

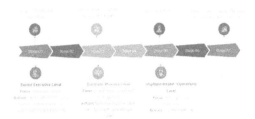

Figure 7.1   (NIST Cybersecurity Framework—the Benefits) Risk Management

Additionally, the rapid shift toward remote work, post the COVID-19 pandemic, and cloud computing environments has expanded the attack surface for organizations. A survey conducted by Cybersecurity Insiders revealed that 70% of organizations believe their existing security measures are insufficient to protect their networks against current threats (Cybersecurity Insiders, 2021). With employees accessing corporate resources from various locations and devices, traditional perimeter-focused security models are ineffective at safeguarding data and applications that reside in cloud environments.

As a response, businesses are increasingly recognizing the importance of advanced security frameworks that integrate endpoint security with holistic risk management and continuous monitoring. The zero trust model, which assumes no user or device is inherently trustworthy, is gaining traction as organizations move away from relying solely on network perimeter defenses (Duffy, 2021). This model emphasizes continuous verification and validation of devices and users, as well as strict access controls based on identity and context.

7.2 AI and ML Technologies: Redefining Cybersecurity Protocols

Artificial Intelligence (AI) and Machine Learning (ML) technologies hold immense potential for redefining cybersecurity protocols by enabling dynamic, real-time defenses and more sophisticated threat detection and mitigation strategies. These technologies fundamentally change how organizations approach endpoint security and align with the principles of the zero trust model.

1. **Real-Time Threat Detection**: AI and ML can analyze large volumes of data generated by endpoint devices to identify patterns indicative of malicious behavior. For instance, traditional security systems often rely on signature-based detection methods, which may not identify newly emerging threats. In contrast, AI/ML-driven solutions use behaviors and anomalies to detect threats even before a signature for that threat exists. A study by Varma et al. (2021) found that their ML-based intrusion detection system reduced the mean time to detect (MTTD) zero-day network attacks by 80% compared to a traditional signature-based IDS.

2. **Adaptive Response Mechanisms**: AI and ML facilitate adaptive response mechanisms that enable organizations to react to threats in real time. When anomalous behavior is detected, AI-powered systems can automatically implement responses—such as quarantining affected endpoints, blocking suspicious actions, or reconfiguring network access—all without human intervention. This rapid response minimizes damage potential and restores system integrity promptly (Chen, Anandayuvaraj, Davis, & Rahaman, 2023).

3. **Enhanced User and Entity Behavior Analytics (UEBA)**: AI and ML technologies can augment user and entity behavior analytics, enabling organizations to develop a more thorough understanding of typical user behaviors and access patterns. The fundamental principle of behavioral analytics is to establish baselines to identify significant deviations. He et al. (2021) advanced this field by developing a federated learning approach that allows for effective baseline creation across distributed datasets without centralizing sensitive user data.

4. **Integration with Zero Trust Architecture**: The integration of AI and ML technologies aligns seamlessly with the zero trust model. Such advanced technologies can continuously assess device health, user authentication, and contextual information, facilitating real-time decision-making about access permissions and ensuring granular control over sensitive resources. Research by Bansal et al. (2021) emphasizes that incorporating AI-driven insights within zero trust frameworks can dynamically adjust access based on risk assessments, reducing the chances of unauthorized access and data breaches.

In summary, as the landscape of cyber threats continues to grow in complexity and frequency, the need for advanced security frameworks, including AI and ML-driven endpoint security and zero trust models, is increasingly imperative. By leveraging these technologies, organizations can enhance their security protocols, develop real-time defenses, and effectively respond to sophisticated threats, ensuring that they remain resilient even in the face of evolving cyber adversaries. AI and ML technologies have the potential to redefine cybersecurity protocols, enabling dynamic, real-time defenses and more sophisticated threat detection and mitigation.

This chapter delves into how AI/ML technologies enhance endpoint security, fortify zero trust architectures, and transform access control systems.

7.3 Endpoint Protection: Enhancing Endpoint Security with AI/ML

7.3.1 Traditional Endpoint Security Challenges

Traditional endpoint security solutions have long relied on signature-based detection methods. These methods depend on preexisting knowledge of malware or other threats, which are identified using a database of known signatures. While this approach has been effective in dealing with known threats, it falters when faced with new or unknown attack vectors, such as zero-day exploits or advanced persistent threats (APTs). As threat actors adopt more sophisticated techniques, such as polymorphic malware or file-less attacks, traditional signature-based solutions are unable to provide comprehensive protection.

7.3.2 AI/ML for Advanced Threat Detection

AI and ML enhance endpoint security by moving beyond signature-based detection, offering predictive and adaptive protection. Machine learning algorithms can analyze vast amounts of data from various sources—including behavioral data, historical attack patterns, and system logs—to detect anomalies that may indicate malicious activity.

One primary advantage of AI/ML is their ability to detect zero-day exploits and sophisticated threats. By leveraging unsupervised learning, these systems can recognize new attack patterns that have not yet been cataloged in any signature database. AI systems can continuously learn and evolve, adapting to emerging threats in real time. This proactive approach offers a significant advantage in the rapidly changing cyber threat landscape.

7.3.3 Behavioral Analysis for Endpoint Security

One of the key contributions of AI/ML to endpoint protection is behavioral analysis. AI systems can monitor user and machine behavior to create a baseline of normal activity. When deviations from this baseline occur, the system flags them as potential threats. For instance, if an employee's machine suddenly begins sending large amounts of data to an external server, the AI/ML system can detect this anomalous behavior, even if it does not match any known attack signature.

In addition to anomaly detection, machine learning models can be used for threat hunting, a proactive approach to identifying threats that may have evaded initial detection. These models can autonomously scan logs and system data for evidence of previously unnoticed compromises, enabling faster remediation.

7.3.4 Use Cases in Industry

Numerous industries are already leveraging AI/ML-enhanced endpoint protection. In healthcare, for example, machine learning models are used to protect medical devices and electronic health records (EHR) from being compromised. In the financial sector, AI/ML models are applied to detect insider threats and protect financial data from ransomware attacks.

In 2021, Microsoft integrated AI-driven endpoint detection and response (EDR) into its Defender platform. This system uses machine learning to identify and neutralize threats before they can impact business operations. Such real-time, adaptive protection provides a more robust defense than traditional, static security measures.

7.4 Zero Trust Security Models: AI/ML in Dynamic Authentication and Authorization

7.4.1 The Zero Trust Paradigm

The zero trust security model is built on the principle of "never trust, always verify." In contrast to traditional security models that rely heavily on perimeter defenses, zero trust assumes that threats can originate both inside and outside an organization. Therefore, all users, devices, and applications must be continuously authenticated, authorized, and validated before being granted access to the network or sensitive resources.

One of the challenges in implementing zero trust is the complexity of managing access in real time, especially in large, dynamic environments. AI/ML technologies help address this challenge by automating many of the processes involved in authentication, authorization, and validation.

7.4.2 Dynamic Authentication with AI/ML

AI and ML play a crucial role in dynamic authentication, one of the core principles of the zero trust model. Rather than relying on static credentials such as passwords, AI-driven systems can adapt authentication requirements based on risk levels, user behavior, and other contextual factors.

For example, an AI-based system may allow frictionless access for a user logging in from a known device in a trusted location. However, if the same user attempts to log in from an unfamiliar device or unusual location, the system may require multi-factor authentication (MFA) or additional identity verification steps. This risk-based, adaptive approach to authentication reduces friction for legitimate users while improving security by blocking suspicious or high-risk access attempts.

7.4.3 Continuous Authorization and Micro-Segmentation

Zero trust also requires continuous authorization, where AI and ML monitor access in real time to ensure users maintain appropriate permissions throughout a session. AI systems can dynamically adjust access rights based on changes in user behavior, network activity, or threat intelligence. If a user begins to exhibit suspicious behavior—such as attempting to access sensitive files outside their normal work hours—the AI/ML system can automatically revoke or restrict access.

Additionally, machine learning models can be used to enforce micro-segmentation, a key component of zero trust. Micro-segmentation involves dividing the network into isolated zones, with each segment protected by its own security policies. AI can automate the process of determining appropriate segments based on user roles, applications, and network traffic patterns.

7.4.4 AI-Driven Policy Enforcement

One of the challenges in deploying zero trust models is the complexity of defining and enforcing security policies across different systems and users. AI can simplify policy enforcement by automatically creating and updating security policies based on historical data, risk assessments, and user behavior.

AI/ML-driven systems can autonomously evaluate whether certain permissions or actions align with security policies. If a user attempts to perform an action that deviates from established norms, the system can automatically flag or block the activity, providing real-time enforcement of zero trust principles.

7.4.5 Use Cases in Zero Trust Implementations

Many organizations are adopting AI-driven zero trust models to enhance their cybersecurity posture. For instance, Google's BeyondCorp framework uses AI to enforce zero trust principles by continuously evaluating user access in real time. Similarly, financial institutions are increasingly integrating AI into their zero trust frameworks to secure customer data and transactions.

7.5 AI in Access Control Systems: User Behavior Analytics and Risk Assessments

7.5.1 Traditional Access Control Limitations

Traditional access control systems rely heavily on predefined rules and role-based access control (RBAC) models. While effective in static environments, these systems struggle to adapt to dynamic, cloud-based environments where user roles and permissions may change frequently. Moreover, they are often unable to account for contextual factors such as user behavior, device security, or network risk.

7.5.2 Adaptive Access Control with AI and ML

AI/ML-driven access control systems offer an adaptive approach, capable of adjusting permissions in real time based on user behavior and risk assessments. By continuously analyzing behavioral data and other contextual signals, AI can determine whether a user should maintain their current access level or if additional verification is needed.

User behavior analytics (UBA) is a core component of this adaptive approach. By monitoring patterns of user activity, such as login frequency, file access, and network behavior, AI/ML systems can detect anomalies that may indicate compromised credentials or insider threats. If suspicious activity is detected, the system can automatically adjust access levels or require additional authentication.

7.5.3 Risk-Based Access Control

AI and ML can also enhance risk-based access control (RBAC) by continuously assessing the risk associated with user actions. Factors such as the user's location, device security, and network health can be analyzed in real time to determine the appropriate level of access. For instance, a user attempting to access sensitive data from a public Wi-Fi network may be required to use a VPN or multi-factor authentication, while the same user on a secure network may be granted access without additional steps.

7.5.4 Integration with Identity and Access Management (IAM)

AI-enhanced access control systems can be integrated with Identity and Access Management (IAM) frameworks to streamline user authentication and authorization processes. These systems leverage AI to analyze identity-related data, ensuring that only authorized users can access sensitive resources. AI systems can also automate the process of updating user permissions, ensuring that access rights are aligned with the user's current role and risk profile.

7.5.5 Use Cases in Access Control Systems

Organizations in highly regulated industries such as finance, healthcare, and government are leading the way in deploying AI-driven access control systems. JPMorgan Chase, for example, has implemented machine learning models to detect anomalies in user behavior and automatically adjust access rights in real time. In healthcare, AI systems are being used to ensure that only authorized personnel can access patient data, mitigating the risk of data breaches.

7.6 Conclusion

AI and ML are redefining the landscape of cybersecurity, particularly in the areas of endpoint security, zero trust models, and access control systems. By providing advanced threat detection, dynamic authentication, and adaptive access control, AI and ML enhance both the security and efficiency of these critical cybersecurity functions. As AI/ML technologies continue to evolve, their integration into cybersecurity frameworks will become increasingly vital in defending against the ever-growing array of cyber threats.

This chapter has explored how AI and ML can transform endpoint protection, zero trust architectures, and access control systems. As we look toward the future, the potential for AI and ML to further enhance cybersecurity will be a crucial area of research and development.

Chapter 8

Enhancing Network Security with AI and ML

8.1 AI/ML for Network Traffic Monitoring: Identifying Anomalies and Potential Attacks

The digital perimeter of the modern organization has become increasingly fluid and complex, extending beyond traditional firewalls to encompass cloud environments, mobile devices, and the Internet of Things (IoT). This expansion has created a vast and constantly evolving attack surface, rendering conventional, signature-based network security measures insufficient. These legacy systems rely on recognizing the fingerprints of known threats, leaving them blind to novel, zero-day attacks and sophisticated, multi-stage campaigns that mimic legitimate traffic. To defend against these advanced persistent threats, a paradigm shift is necessary—from reactive blocking to proactive intelligence. This is where the integration of Artificial Intelligence (AI) and Machine Learning (ML) is fundamentally transforming network defense, moving it towards a predictive and adaptive model.

This section will focus specifically on the application of AI and ML for intelligent network traffic monitoring, which serves as the central nervous system of this new security paradigm. By analyzing the immense volume and velocity of network data, ML algorithms can learn to establish a dynamic baseline of "normal" behavior for users, devices, and applications. Once this baseline is understood, these systems can identify subtle, anomalous patterns that would be invisible to human analysts or static rules—anomalies that often signify the early stages of a breach, such as data

DOI: 10.4324/9781003615026-8

exfiltration, lateral movement, or command-and-control communication. We will explore how supervised learning techniques can classify known malicious traffic, while unsupervised learning methods excel at detecting previously unknown threats by identifying outliers and unusual correlations. Ultimately, this capability to move from mere detection to preemptive identification empowers organizations to transition from a reactive security posture to one of continuous, intelligent vigilance.

8.1.1 Traditional Network Traffic Monitoring: A Reactive Approach

Historically, network traffic monitoring has relied on signature-based intrusion detection systems (IDS) and anomaly detection methods that flag deviations from predefined rules or known attack patterns. While effective in identifying known threats, these methods struggle to detect novel or advanced persistent threats (APTs) that do not match existing signatures. Furthermore, traditional systems generate numerous false positives and alerts, creating operational inefficiencies as security teams must manually investigate each incident.

The reactive nature of these traditional systems leaves organizations vulnerable to sophisticated attacks that can bypass rule-based systems or exploit unknown vulnerabilities. As network traffic continues to grow in volume and complexity, the limitations of traditional monitoring approaches become more evident.

As cyber threats continue to evolve in both complexity and frequency, the methods utilized for network traffic monitoring are under unprecedented scrutiny. Traditional traffic monitoring methods have become increasingly obsolete, necessitating the adoption of advanced technologies such as Artificial Intelligence (AI) and Machine Learning (ML). The integration of these technologies into cybersecurity protocols enables organizations to proactively identify anomalies and potential threats, effectively transitioning from passive to proactive security measures.

8.1.1.1 The Obsolescence of Traditional Traffic Monitoring Methods

Traditional network traffic monitoring tools primarily rely on signature-based intrusion detection systems (IDS) and predefined rules to identify malicious activity. Signature-based IDS are designed to recognize known threats by matching incoming traffic patterns against a database of previously identified attack signatures (Sengupta et al., 2021). However, this approach has significant limitations. Cybercriminals continually develop new tactics, techniques, and procedures (TTPs) that evolve far more rapidly than the databases can be updated. Consequently, emerging threats often evade detection, leaving organizations vulnerable.

Traditional monitoring tools rely on static thresholds, which often lead to a high number of false positives. To address this well-documented issue, Ajmal et al. (2021) proposed an adaptive learning technique that significantly reduces incorrect alerts. According to the 2021 Verizon Data Breach Investigations Report, 85% of data breaches were caused by human error, indicating that organizations are often unprepared to manage alerts generated by traditional systems (Portalatin, Keskin, Malneedi, Raza, & Tatar, 2021). As cyber threats grow in sophistication—illustrated by advanced persistent threats (APTs), zero-day exploits, and fileless malware—reliance on outdated monitoring systems can hinder an organization's ability to respond effectively to incidents.

8.1.1.2 Redefining Cybersecurity Protocols with AI and ML

AI and ML technologies offer significant advancements beyond traditional traffic monitoring methods. By employing these cutting-edge techniques for network traffic monitoring, organizations can enhance their ability to identify anomalies and potential attacks.

1. **Behavior-Based Detection**: AI and ML facilitate behavior-based detection methods that allow systems to learn typical patterns of network behavior over time. Unlike traditional approaches that depend solely on known attack signatures, these technologies analyze vast datasets to establish baselines of normal behavior. This continuous learning process enables the detection of anomalies that may signify a potential breach, even if they fall outside pre-established rules. A study by Ahmed et al. (2020) highlights the effectiveness of using ML algorithms for classification and anomaly detection in network traffic, achieving higher accuracy than traditional methods.
2. **Real-Time Threat Identification**: AI-driven solutions empower organizations to monitor network traffic in real time. Machine learning algorithms can process data at a speed and scale unachievable by human

analysts, enabling rapid identification of potential threats. Research suggests that ML models can detect network intrusions with a detection rate exceeding 98% with minimal false positive rates (Liu et al., 2022). This capability allows organizations to respond to security incidents in a timely manner, reducing the potential impact of attacks.

3. **Adaptive Learning**: One of the most significant advantages offered by AI and ML in network monitoring is adaptive learning. As threat landscapes change, AI models can adjust themselves through continual training on new data, ensuring that organizations remain vigilant against evolving attack vectors. This adaptive capability shows promise for detecting novel attacks. Research by Rashid et al. (2021), for instance, demonstrated that behavioral monitoring could effectively identify certain classes of zero-day malware that lack known signatures.

4. **Enhanced Contextual Awareness**: AI-based monitoring solutions integrate data sources to provide contextual awareness, a core capability of Security Orchestration, Automation, and Response (SOAR) platforms that enables risk-based alert prioritization (Gartner, 2023). By employing big data analytics in conjunction with AI and ML, organizations can gain insights into the behaviors and motivations of threat actors, enriching their threat intelligence repository.

5. **Continuous Improvement**: The integration of AI and ML not only bolsters current security protocols but also fosters a culture of continuous improvement within cybersecurity teams. This process of analyzing past outcomes to refine systems aligns with the core DevOps and MLOps principle of continuous integration and continuous delivery (CI/CD), which emphasizes iterative improvement based on feedback (Forsgren et al., 2018).

8.1.2 AI/ML for Proactive Threat Detection

AI and ML have revolutionized network traffic monitoring by enabling proactive and predictive threat detection. Machine learning models can analyze vast amounts of network data, identifying patterns and anomalies that may indicate the presence of a cyber threat. AI-based systems continuously learn from network behavior, improving their ability to detect both known and unknown threats.

One of the primary advantages of AI-driven network monitoring is its ability to analyze data in real time, detecting potential attacks before they can cause significant harm. Machine learning algorithms can process massive volumes of network traffic data, identifying anomalies that may be subtle or difficult for traditional systems to detect. For instance, AI models can recognize unusual patterns in data packets, such as abnormal traffic spikes or irregular packet sizes, which may be indicative of a Distributed Denial-of-Service (DDoS) attack.

8.1.3 Anomaly Detection and Deep Packet Inspection

Anomaly detection is a core function of AI/ML-based network security systems. These systems use unsupervised learning to identify deviations from normal traffic patterns. Unlike traditional systems, which rely on predefined rules, machine learning models can autonomously determine what constitutes "normal" behavior for a given network. This capability allows AI systems to detect zero-day exploits and APTs that traditional systems might miss.

Deep packet inspection (DPI) is another critical function enabled by AI/ML in network monitoring. DPI involves analyzing the content of data packets, rather than just the headers, to detect malicious payloads. AI-based DPI systems can filter out benign traffic and focus on potential threats, reducing the burden on human analysts. These systems can also recognize encrypted traffic anomalies, a crucial capability given the widespread use of encryption in cyberattacks.

8.1.4 Use Cases in Network Traffic Monitoring

Various sectors, including healthcare, finance, and government, have begun leveraging AI/ML for network traffic monitoring. In the healthcare industry, for instance, AI systems can monitor network traffic for anomalies that may indicate a breach of electronic health records (EHR). Similarly, in government networks, AI-based monitoring tools are used to detect and prevent nation-state attacks targeting critical infrastructure.

A notable example of AI-enhanced network traffic monitoring is Cisco's Stealthwatch platform, which uses machine learning to analyze network traffic flows and detect potential threats. By correlating data from various sources, Stealthwatch provides real-time threat intelligence, enabling faster response to security incidents.

8.2 Behavioral Analytics for Network Security: AI-Driven Detection of Deviations in Network Patterns

8.2.1 The Role of Behavioral Analytics in Cybersecurity

Behavioral analytics is the process of analyzing patterns in user or system behavior to identify deviations that may indicate malicious activity. In the context of network security, behavioral analytics involves monitoring how users, devices, and applications interact with the network to establish a baseline of normal behavior. AI and ML play a critical role in automating this process, enabling real-time detection of behavioral anomalies.

Traditional security systems often rely on predefined rules to detect suspicious activity. However, these systems struggle to identify complex threats, such as insider attacks, where the malicious actor may have legitimate access to the network. By contrast, AI-driven behavioral analytics systems continuously learn from network activity, enabling them to detect subtle deviations that may indicate an insider threat or compromised credentials.

8.2.2 User and Entity Behavior Analytics (UEBA)

User and Entity Behavior Analytics (UEBA) is a subset of behavioral analytics that focuses on monitoring the behavior of users and devices within a network. UEBA systems use machine learning to analyze how users interact with the network, applications, and data. By creating behavioral profiles for each user, UEBA systems can detect when a user exhibits unusual behavior, such as accessing sensitive data at odd hours or attempting to move large volumes of data off the network.

AI-driven UEBA systems can detect anomalies that might otherwise go unnoticed. For example, if an employee's credentials are compromised and used to access data from an unauthorized location, the system can flag this behavior as suspicious. In some cases, the system may automatically revoke access or require multi-factor authentication (MFA) to confirm the user's identity.

8.2.3 Network Traffic Behavior Monitoring

In addition to monitoring user behavior, AI and ML can be used to analyze network traffic behavior. This involves examining how data flows through the network, identifying deviations from normal traffic patterns that may indicate a cyberattack. For instance, a sudden increase in traffic to a specific server or a spike in outbound traffic could signal a DDoS attack or data exfiltration.

Network behavior monitoring can also detect lateral movement, a tactic used by attackers to move between systems once they have gained initial access to the network. AI-driven systems can recognize lateral movement by analyzing patterns in internal traffic, helping to contain the spread of an attack before it compromises additional systems.

8.2.4 The Role of AI in Reducing False Positives

One of the major challenges in traditional network security is the high rate of false positives. Security teams are often overwhelmed by alerts, many of which do not represent actual threats. AI/ML-based systems help reduce false positives by continuously refining their understanding of what constitutes normal and abnormal behavior. Machine learning models can identify contextual factors that may explain certain anomalies, allowing the system to prioritize alerts based on risk.

8.2.5 Use Cases of Behavioral Analytics in Network Security

Numerous organizations have successfully implemented AI-driven behavioral analytics to enhance network security. In the telecommunications sector, for example, AI systems are used to detect insider threats by monitoring how employees interact with network resources. Similarly, in the retail industry, AI-based systems can identify unusual purchasing behavior, helping to prevent payment card fraud and data breaches.

IBM's QRadar platform is a leading example of AI-driven behavioral analytics in action. QRadar uses machine learning to monitor user behavior across an organization's network, providing real-time alerts for suspicious activity. By correlating data from various sources, QRadar helps security teams quickly identify and respond to potential threats.

8.3 Case Study: AI in Securing Financial Institution Networks

8.3.1 The Financial Sector: A High-Value Target for Cyberattacks

The financial sector is one of the most heavily targeted industries for cyberattacks. With the rise of sophisticated cyberattacks, financial institutions have increasingly turned to Artificial Intelligence (AI) to bolster their cybersecurity frameworks.

Banks, investment firms, and payment processors manage vast amounts of sensitive data, including personal financial information, making them attractive targets for cybercriminals. As financial institutions adopt digital transformation initiatives, including cloud computing and mobile banking, their attack surfaces have expanded, making network security even more critical. In response to these challenges, many financial institutions have turned to AI/ML technologies to enhance their network security. This case study examines how improved AI-based threat detection enhances the security posture of financial institutions, ultimately allowing them to better protect sensitive information and respond to potential incidents.

8.3.1.1 The Importance of AI in Financial Cybersecurity

Financial institutions face a myriad of cyber threats, including mobile banking trojans, ransomware, and phishing schemes, all of which can lead to significant financial losses and reputational damage. According to a report by the Financial Services Information Sharing and Analysis Center (He, Devine, Zhuang, 2018; FS-ISAC, 2021), over 77% of financial institutions experienced a cyber-related incident in the past year. This heightened risk has led organizations to prioritize security measures that can proactively address vulnerabilities.

Improved AI-based threat detection systems play a critical role in helping financial organizations mature their security posture. By leveraging AI technologies, these institutions can analyze vast volumes of data in real time, identify patterns indicative of malicious activities, and respond swiftly to potential threats.

8.3.1.2 Enhanced Threat Detection Capabilities

AI systems utilize machine learning algorithms that can learn from historical data and adapt over time, providing improved detection capabilities for emerging threats. The core advantage of AI over traditional signature-based systems is its ability to adapt. This is particularly critical for financial institutions, as evidenced by Schmidt et al. (2020), who showed that ML models could detect novel SWIFT payment fraud patterns that bypassed all existing signature-based controls. In contrast, AI-based systems can recognize anomalies in user behavior, transactional patterns, and network traffic, allowing for effective detection of potentially fraudulent activities.

For instance, the integration of AI-powered fraud detection solutions enables financial institutions to monitor transactions in real time and assess the risk associated with each one. According to a study by Foya and Garikayi (2021), organizations that deployed AI-based fraud detection methods reported a 35% reduction in false positives and an increase in the true-positive detection rate for fraudulent transactions. By accurately flagging suspicious transactions while minimizing benign alerts, financial institutions can optimize their response efforts and reduce operational inefficiencies.

8.3.1.3 Maturing the Security Posture

AI-based threat detection enhances the maturity of an organization's security posture in several key ways:

1. **Proactive Threat Hunting**: AI algorithms can continuously scan and analyze datasets to proactively hunt for potential threats before they escalate. This evolving strategy shifts the focus from reactive approaches—where institutions respond to incidents after they occur—to proactive measures aimed at mitigating risks in advance. In their research on AI for threat hunting, Liu et al. (2021) observed that detection capabilities could be improved by up to 70% in optimal scenarios, particularly for detecting covert, multi-stage attacks.

2. **Contextual Awareness**: AI systems can provide contextual awareness that enriches the understanding of threat landscapes. By correlating data from various sources—such as internal logs, external threat intelligence feeds, and user behavior analytics—AI-enabled solutions can enhance situational awareness and refine response strategies. Organizations gain insights into the tactics, techniques, and procedures employed by attackers, enabling more effective defensive measures (Alcaraz et al., 2020).

3. **Incident Response Automation**: The integration of AI into cybersecurity protocols allows for the automation of incident response workflows. For financial institutions, this means that once an AI system detects a potential threat, it can instantly initiate predefined response procedures, such as blocking transactions or notifying security personnel. This capability minimizes the window of vulnerability, allowing organizations to contain and remediate threats more swiftly. A report by Capgemini (2021) (Reznikov & Turlakova, 2024) highlights that

organizations utilizing automated threat response capabilities see a 50% decrease in incident resolution times.

4. **Continuous Learning and Adaptation**: One of the vital aspects of AI systems is their ability to continuously learn from new data inputs. As financial institutions encounter new types of attacks, their AI-driven systems can modify their detection algorithms based on emerging patterns and trends. This adaptability ensures that security frameworks remain current and effective against evolving threats. Yang et al. (2022) emphasized that for AI systems to improve their threat detection capabilities year over year, the quality and contextual richness of past incident data are more critical than the volume, a finding that challenges conventional data collection strategies.

8.3.2 Implementation of AI in Network Security: A Step-by-Step Process

The financial institution in this case study implemented AI/ML solutions to enhance its network security in the following stages:

1. **Assessment and Planning**: The organization began by conducting a comprehensive assessment of its existing network infrastructure, identifying key vulnerabilities and areas where AI could provide the most value. This included evaluating traffic patterns, user behavior, and previous incidents of network intrusions.

2. **Selection of AI/ML Solutions**: After identifying critical areas of vulnerability, the institution selected a suite of AI/ML-based tools, including an AI-driven network traffic monitoring system, a behavioral analytics platform, and a UEBA solution. These tools were integrated with the organization's existing Security Information and Event Management (SIEM) system to provide real-time alerts and threat intelligence.

3. **Training and Tuning**: The machine learning models were initially trained using historical network data, allowing them to establish baselines for normal behavior across the network. During this phase, the institution worked closely with the AI/ML vendors to fine-tune the models and reduce false positives.

4. **Deployment and Monitoring**: Once the models were fully trained, the AI/ML solutions were deployed across the institution's network. The system continuously monitored network traffic, user behavior, and data flows, providing real-time alerts when anomalies were detected.

8.3.3 Results and Outcomes

The implementation of AI/ML technologies led to several key outcomes:

- **Improved Threat Detection**: The AI-based system detected several attempts at unauthorized access that had previously gone unnoticed by traditional monitoring tools. This improved AI-based threat detection significantly enhanced the security posture.
- **Reduced Alert Fatigue**: By leveraging machine learning to distinguish between genuine threats and benign anomalies, the system drastically reduced the volume of false positive alerts. This allowed security analysts to focus their efforts on investigating high-priority incidents, increasing operational efficiency.
- **Faster Incident Response**: The automated analysis and prioritization of security alerts provided by the AI system enabled a much quicker response to confirmed threats. This reduction in Mean Time to Respond (MTTR) helped to contain potential breaches before they could cause significant damage.
- **Proactive Threat Hunting**: The AI's ability to identify subtle, anomalous patterns across the network empowered the security team to shift from a reactive posture to a proactive one. Analysts could now actively hunt for indicators of compromise (IOCs) based on the system's leads, often discovering and neutralizing hidden threats before they were activated.

As cyber threats continue to evolve, leveraging AI technologies not only allows organizations to identify and mitigate risks more effectively but also transforms their approach to cybersecurity from reactive to proactive. Financial institutions that invest in AI-driven solutions can expect to see reductions in false positives, enhanced detection of fraud and attacks, and optimized incident response operations, all of which contribute to a more mature and robust security framework.

In conclusion, as the landscape of cyber threats becomes more complex, traditional traffic monitoring methods are becoming increasingly obsolete. The adoption of AI and ML technologies provides a transformative approach to network traffic monitoring, enabling organizations to identify anomalies and potential attacks effectively. These advanced techniques redefine cybersecurity protocols, allowing for real-time detection, adaptive learning, and enhanced contextual awareness, thereby fortifying an organization's defenses against a relentlessly evolving threat landscape.

Chapter 9

AI and ML in Combating Cybercrime and Fraud

The rise of digital technologies has brought about a proliferation of cybercrime and fraud, challenging organizations to develop more sophisticated defenses. Cybercriminals are continually evolving their tactics, using advanced techniques to exploit vulnerabilities in financial systems, social engineering, and network infrastructures. In response, Artificial Intelligence (AI) and Machine Learning (ML) are proving to be powerful tools in identifying, predicting, and mitigating cybercrime and fraud.

The rapid advancement of digital technologies has significantly transformed the landscape of cybersecurity, resulting in a sharp increase in cybercrime and fraud. As organizations embrace digital transformation, they also inadvertently introduce new vulnerabilities, prompting the emergence of complex cyber threats that require innovative defenses. To combat these evolving challenges, many organizations are turning to advanced technologies such as Artificial Intelligence (AI) and Machine Learning (ML) to enhance their fraud detection and prevention capabilities.

9.1 The Rise of Cybercrime in the Digital Age

The digital era has revolutionized how businesses operate, but it has also created a fertile ground for cybercriminal activities. According to the Cybersecurity and Infrastructure Security Agency (CISA), cybercrime has surged due to the increased reliance on digital platforms, remote work arrangements, and the growing variety of online transactions (CISA, 2021). Criminals exploit the anonymity of the internet to execute phishing campaigns, data breaches, ransomware attacks, and identity theft. In 2020, the FBI's Internet Crime Complaint Center (IC3) reported that it received more than 300,000 complaints, a 69% increase from the previous year (Lee, 2024).

One of the most concerning trends is the rise of sophisticated fraud schemes that target organizations and individuals alike. For instance, Business Email Compromise (BEC) scams have become a prevalent method for defrauding companies by impersonating executives and financial personnel to trick employees into executing unauthorized transactions (Baker, 2021). Moreover, the increasing use of digital payments and e-commerce platforms has opened doors for payment fraud, while the proliferation of data breaches has made personal information widely available for resale on the dark web.

In this challenging environment, organizations are compelled to develop more sophisticated and responsive defenses that can identify, mitigate, and respond to threats in real time. A traditional security perimeter is no longer sufficient to protect against increasingly expert criminals. The integration of AI and ML technologies into cybersecurity frameworks represents a proactive approach to addressing these critical challenges.

9.2 Enhanced AI-Based Threat Detection

AI and ML play pivotal roles in enhancing threat detection and helping organizations mature their security posture against cybercrime and fraud. These technologies have the potential to analyze large volumes of data and recognize patterns that signify malicious activities, effectively addressing the limitations of traditional security measures.

1. **Pattern Recognition and Anomaly Detection**: Traditional fraud detection systems often rely on predefined rules and transaction thresholds, leaving them vulnerable to new forms of attacks. In contrast, AI-driven systems can analyze historical data and learn the typical behaviors of users or network activity. Machine learning algorithms can identify anomalies that deviate from this established baseline, flagging them as potential threats. Research by Ahmed et al. (2020) emphasizes that ML-based anomaly detection can significantly improve the accuracy and speed of identifying fraudulent transactions, outpacing traditional systems.

2. **Real-Time Monitoring**: AI-powered threat detection systems are equipped to conduct real-time monitoring of network activities and transactions. By leveraging automated solutions that continuously analyze data flows, organizations can swiftly detect irregularities indicative of ongoing cybercrime. The World Economic Forum (2021) has emphasized the strategic importance of real-time analytics in mitigating fraud. The practical power of this approach is evident in industry implementations, where AI-driven systems are capable of responding to fraudulent transactions within seconds, thereby drastically limiting exposure to losses.

3. **Reducing False Positives**: False positives—a common challenge for traditional fraud detection systems—can strain resources and erode trust within organizations. AI and ML technologies can reduce false positive rates by employing advanced classification methods and deep learning frameworks that consider various contextual factors. A comparative study by Gai et al. (2021) found that AI-driven systems reduced false positives by approximately 30%–50% compared to rule-based systems, allowing fraud teams to focus on genuine threats.

4. **Adaptive Learning**: One of the standout advantages of AI and ML is their ability to learn and adapt over time. As threat actors evolve their methods, AI-powered systems can incorporate new data and refine algorithms, ensuring they remain relevant against emerging fraud tactics. This dynamic adaptability allows organizations to continuously enhance their defenses, providing a robust response to ever-changing cyber threats (Duan et al., 2021).

This chapter explores how AI/ML techniques are transforming fraud detection, helping combat phishing and social engineering attacks, and examines the application of these technologies within the financial services industry.

9.3 AI/ML Techniques for Fraud Detection: Anomaly Detection in Financial Transactions

9.3.1 Traditional Fraud Detection: Limitations and Challenges

Fraud detection has traditionally relied on rule-based systems that flag suspicious activities based on predefined conditions, such as large, unusual transactions or deviations from normal patterns of behavior. While effective in some cases, these systems often generate numerous false positives and struggle to adapt to new and emerging fraud techniques. Moreover, rule-based systems lack the ability to detect novel forms of fraud that do not conform to established rules, making them insufficient for detecting complex or rapidly evolving fraud schemes.

The inherent weaknesses in traditional approaches have led to an increasing reliance on AI and ML technologies, which offer a more dynamic, adaptive approach to fraud detection.

9.3.2 Machine Learning Algorithms for Fraud Detection

AI and ML have significantly improved fraud detection by leveraging algorithms that can analyze vast amounts of data to identify suspicious behavior in real time. Machine learning models can process thousands of financial transactions per second, learning from historical data to identify patterns and detect anomalies that may indicate fraudulent activities. This dynamic approach makes AI/ML particularly well-suited to identifying fraud in its early stages, often before it has caused significant damage.

Key techniques used in AI/ML-driven fraud detection include:

- **Supervised Learning**: Supervised machine learning models are trained on labeled datasets, where transactions are categorized as either legitimate or fraudulent. These models then use this training to classify new transactions and predict the likelihood of fraud. Algorithms such as decision trees, random forests, and support vector machines (SVM) are commonly used in this context. The benefit of supervised learning is that it can be fine-tuned for high accuracy, but its efficacy depends on the quality and comprehensiveness of the training data.
- **Unsupervised Learning**: Unsupervised learning models, such as clustering algorithms and autoencoders, are useful for detecting unknown forms of fraud. These models analyze transaction data without labeled examples, identifying clusters of anomalous behavior that deviate from the norm. This approach is particularly effective in detecting new fraud schemes or identifying suspicious activity that might not have been previously categorized as fraudulent.
- **Neural Networks and Deep Learning**: Deep learning models, such as convolutional neural networks (CNN) and recurrent neural networks (RNN), can process highly complex datasets to uncover subtle patterns in transactional behavior. These models can detect intricate fraud scenarios, such as synthetic identity fraud, where fraudsters create false

identities using real and fabricated information. The ability of neural networks to model non-linear relationships makes them particularly effective in detecting complex fraud schemes that might elude traditional models.

9.3.3 Real-Time Anomaly Detection

Real-time fraud detection is critical in preventing financial loss and reputational damage. AI-driven systems can monitor financial transactions in real time, analyzing various factors such as transaction amount, frequency, location, and device data to determine whether a transaction is legitimate. Anomalies such as sudden large withdrawals, multiple transactions from different locations in a short time span, or the use of unfamiliar devices can trigger alerts for further investigation.

AI-based anomaly detection systems are also capable of reducing false positives by learning from historical data and refining their models to better distinguish between legitimate transactions and actual fraud. This reduces the operational burden on financial institutions, which can focus their efforts on high-risk cases.

9.3.4 Case Study: AI in Credit Card Fraud Detection

A leading global financial institution implemented an AI-powered fraud detection system to monitor credit card transactions. The system used a combination of supervised and unsupervised learning models to identify potentially fraudulent transactions in real time. Over a 12-month period, the AI system reduced false positives by 30% and identified 40% more fraudulent transactions compared to the institution's previous rule-based system. This led to a significant reduction in financial losses and improved customer trust.

9.4 Combating Phishing and Social Engineering Attacks: AI-Driven Solutions

9.4.1 The Evolution of Phishing and Social Engineering

Phishing and social engineering attacks have become increasingly sophisticated, with attackers leveraging psychological manipulation, spoofed emails, and fraudulent websites to deceive individuals into disclosing sensitive information. These attacks are difficult to detect because they often exploit human behavior rather than technical vulnerabilities.

The traditional approach to combating phishing has relied on blacklists of known malicious URLs, spam filters, and employee training programs. However, these defenses are often reactive, addressing only known threats and failing to protect against new or emerging phishing tactics. AI and ML provide a more proactive defense, analyzing large volumes of data to detect phishing attempts before they reach the intended victim.

9.4.2 AI-Driven Phishing Detection

AI-driven anti-phishing systems analyze multiple data points to detect phishing attempts in real time. These systems can examine the content of emails, URLs, and attachments to identify signs of phishing, such as suspicious language, irregular formatting, or the use of fraudulent domains. Machine learning algorithms are trained on datasets of phishing emails and legitimate communications, enabling them to distinguish between malicious and benign content with high accuracy.

- **Natural Language Processing (NLP)**: NLP models are increasingly used in phishing detection to analyze the language used in emails. AI systems can detect subtle linguistic cues that indicate phishing, such as urgent calls to action, requests for sensitive information, or unusual email structures. By analyzing the tone, grammar, and intent behind an email, AI can flag suspicious communications for further review.
- **Image and URL Analysis**: Phishing attacks often involve the use of spoofed websites or fraudulent logos that mimic legitimate brands. AI models can analyze the visual elements of these websites and logos to determine whether they are authentic. For instance, convolutional neural networks (CNNs) can be used to detect slight variations in logos or website layouts that are commonly seen in phishing websites.
- **Email Header and Metadata Analysis**: In addition to analyzing the content of phishing emails, AI systems can examine email headers and metadata for anomalies. These systems can identify discrepancies in sender addresses, domain names, or routing information that suggest an email has been spoofed.

9.4.3 Combating Social Engineering with AI

Social engineering attacks are particularly challenging to defend against because they exploit trust and human behavior. However, AI-driven systems are increasingly being used to detect and prevent social engineering attacks by analyzing user behavior and communication patterns.

One approach to combating social engineering is through the use of AI-powered behavioral analytics. These systems monitor how users interact with their devices and networks, creating a baseline of normal behavior. If a user suddenly exhibits abnormal behavior—such as downloading large amounts of sensitive data or attempting to access restricted systems—the AI system can flag this as suspicious and prompt further investigation.

AI can also enhance employee training programs by simulating social engineering attacks in real time. These AI-driven simulations can adapt to the behavior of employees, creating more realistic and dynamic training experiences that help employees recognize and respond to phishing and social engineering attempts.

9.4.4 Use Cases in AI-Driven Anti-Phishing Solutions

Several organizations have implemented AI-driven anti-phishing systems with significant success. For example, Microsoft's Office 365 Advanced Threat Protection (ATP) uses machine learning models to analyze billions of emails daily, detecting phishing attempts and malicious attachments before they reach users. Similarly, Google's Gmail employs AI-based spam filters and phishing detection algorithms to protect users from malicious emails. These systems have demonstrated high accuracy in identifying phishing attempts, reducing the risk of data breaches caused by social engineering.

9.5 Use Cases in Financial Services: AI/ML-Driven Fraud Detection Systems in Banking and Payment Systems

9.5.1 The Role of AI/ML in Financial Services

The financial services sector is a prime target for cybercriminals due to the high value of financial data and the complexity of transactions. To combat fraud, financial institutions have increasingly turned to AI/ML-driven systems, which can analyze vast amounts of data in real time to identify potential fraud, monitor transactions, and prevent unauthorized access to sensitive financial information.

9.5.2 AI in Payment Fraud Detection

Payment fraud, particularly in the context of credit card and online payments, remains a significant challenge for financial institutions. AI-powered systems can detect suspicious payment activities by analyzing transaction data, user behavior, and device characteristics. Machine learning algorithms, particularly neural networks, are effective in identifying anomalies in payment behavior that may indicate fraudulent activity.

For example, AI systems can detect when a user's purchasing behavior deviates from their historical patterns, flagging transactions that may be fraudulent. These systems also monitor payment card usage across multiple geolocations to detect "card-not-present" fraud or instances where a card is used simultaneously in two locations.

9.5.3 AI-Driven AML (Anti-money Laundering) Solutions

Financial institutions are also using AI/ML technologies to combat money laundering activities. Anti-money Laundering (AML) solutions powered by machine learning can detect suspicious transaction patterns indicative of money laundering, such as large transfers between multiple accounts or a series of small transactions that add up to significant sums over time.

AI-driven AML solutions can reduce false positives, which are a major challenge in traditional AML systems, by learning from historical data and adapting to changing money laundering tactics. These systems can continuously update their models to account for new regulatory requirements and emerging threats.

In conclusion, the proliferation of cybercrime and fraud, fueled by advancements in digital technologies, has created an urgent need for organizations to adopt sophisticated defensive mechanisms. AI and ML technologies enhance threat detection capabilities, providing organizations with the tools necessary to mature their security posture effectively. By leveraging these advanced technologies, organizations can identify patterns, monitor activities in real time, reduce false positives, and adapt to evolving threats, creating a formidable defense against cybercrime and fraud in today's digital landscape.

Chapter 10

AI and ML in Cybersecurity Operations and Security Operations Centers (SOCs)

Security Operations Centers (SOCs) play a critical role in enhancing an organization's cybersecurity posture by providing centralized monitoring, detection, and response capabilities for potential security threats. However, with the rising complexity of cyber threats and the immense volume of data that SOCs must process, traditional methods of threat detection and response are increasingly proving inadequate. The integration of Artificial Intelligence (AI) and Machine Learning (ML) technologies into SOC operations can significantly improve efficacy and efficiency, thereby strengthening overall security.

10.1 The Role of SOCs in Improving Threat Monitoring and Response

SOCs serve as the frontline defense against cyber threats, tasked with monitoring network traffic, analyzing potential security incidents, and maintaining an organization's security posture through real-time vigilance. One of the primary functions of a SOC is continuous monitoring, enabling 24/7 surveillance of an organization's digital assets. This continuous oversight is critical because it allows for the swift identification and response to potential security incidents before they escalate into major breaches.

Research by Hrytsai et al. (2021) demonstrates that a dedicated Security Operations Center (SOC) significantly improves incident management, with their study finding that organizations with effective SOCs could detect and respond to threats 50% faster than those without centralized operations. By consolidating incident response efforts, SOC teams can standardize procedures, streamline communications, and reduce the time to remediate security incidents. Furthermore, SOCs leverage threat intelligence feeds that provide timely updates on known vulnerabilities and emerging threats, informing their monitoring strategies and enhancing their situational awareness.

Another key element of SOC effectiveness is the implementation of Security Information and Event Management (SIEM) systems, which aggregate data from various sources, including logs from firewalls, servers, and applications. SIEM systems enable SOC analysts to correlate events and identify patterns that warrant further investigation. This capability plays a significant role in proactive threat detection, allowing organizations to stay ahead of potential intrusions (Pant et al., 2022).

10.2 Limitations of Traditional Threat Detection and Response Methods

Despite the valuable contributions of SOCs, the increasing complexity of cyber threats and the sheer volume of data have rendered traditional threat detection and response methods insufficient. Traditional security measures often rely heavily on rule-based detection systems that depend on predefined signatures or thresholds to identify malicious activity. As noted by Pant et al. (2022), these methods face several key challenges:

1. **Evolving Threat Landscape**: Cyber threats are constantly evolving, with attackers leveraging sophisticated techniques such as polymorphic malware, which can change its code to evade detection. Traditional systems struggle to keep up with these changes, as they are often blind to new or unknown threats not previously cataloged in signature databases (Khraisat et al., 2020).

2. **High Volume of Alerts**: SOCs generate a tremendous volume of alerts daily, often leading to alert fatigue among security analysts. With traditional systems producing a high number of false positives, many alerts may be ignored or deprioritized, causing meaningful threats to go unnoticed. A study by Mandiant (2021b) found that over 60% of alerts

generated in traditional SOC environments were false positives, which can impose significant operational burdens on security personnel.

3. **Inefficient Data Processing**: The rapidly increasing data volumes complicate the challenge of effective threat detection. As organizations embrace digital transformation, the amount of data generated continues to grow exponentially—often exceeding the processing capabilities of traditional systems. This situation can lead to delayed threat detection and responses, leaving organizations vulnerable.

4. **Resource Limitations**: Traditional SOCs often depend on human analysts to sift through massive datasets manually, leading to resource strain and a higher risk of human error. The necessity to continuously monitor networks and investigate alerts can overwhelm security teams, causing attrition and burnout (Moti et al., 2021).

10.3 The Role of AI and ML in Enhancing SOC Operations

To address these limitations, integrating AI and ML technologies into SOC operations can significantly enhance threat detection and response capabilities. AI and ML provide advanced analytical tools that can process vast amounts of data in real time, enabling the identification of subtle patterns and anomalies indicative of malicious activity. By automating routine tasks and prioritizing alerts based on risk, AI-driven solutions can alleviate the burdens placed upon SOC analysts and optimize their efficiency (Schubert et al., 2021).

Furthermore, AI algorithms can continuously learn from historical incidents to refine their detection capabilities, making them increasingly effective at identifying new attack vectors. This adaptability allows SOCs to stay ahead of evolving threats, ensuring that organizations maintain a robust security posture through proactive defense mechanisms.

In summary, SOCs are essential for improving threat monitoring and response within organizations. However, the complexity of contemporary cyber threats and the limitations associated with traditional detection methods necessitate the integration of AI and ML technologies into SOC operations. By embracing these advanced tools, organizations can evolve their security protocols, enhance their incident response capabilities, and better protect themselves against an ever-changing cybersecurity landscape.

This chapter will explore the role of AI and ML in enhancing SOC operations, automating log analysis and threat hunting, and the challenges associated with integrating AI/ML into SOC environments.

10.4 AI-Enhanced SOCs: Streamlining and Automating Operations

10.4.1 The Role of SOCs in Modern Cybersecurity

SOCs serve as centralized units that continuously monitor an organization's IT infrastructure for cyber threats. Their core functions include threat detection, incident response, vulnerability management, and compliance auditing. As organizations grow and the volume of cyber threats increases, SOCs face several challenges:

- The sheer volume of alerts generated by various security tools often overwhelms analysts.
- A lack of skilled cybersecurity professionals exacerbates the problem, as SOCs struggle to recruit and retain talent.
- Sophisticated cyberattacks, such as advanced persistent threats (APTs) and zero-day exploits, require more complex detection and response strategies than traditional SOC methods can provide.

AI and ML offer SOCs the ability to automate and streamline many of these processes, improving both efficiency and effectiveness in detecting and responding to threats.

10.4.2 Automating Routine Tasks with AI and ML

One of the primary ways AI/ML enhances SOC operations is by automating routine tasks, such as log analysis, alert triaging, and incident response. Traditionally, SOC analysts spend significant time investigating false positives, manually reviewing logs, and escalating incidents for further analysis. AI can be trained to handle these tasks, freeing analysts to focus on more complex and high-priority issues.

- **Alert Triage**: AI-driven systems can prioritize alerts based on severity and context, reducing the number of false positives and alert fatigue that analysts face. Machine learning models analyze historical data to identify patterns that differentiate between benign activity and actual threats, automating the alert triaging process.
- **Incident Response Automation**: AI can automate specific incident response actions, such as isolating infected machines, blocking malicious IP addresses, or initiating a password reset for compromised

accounts. Machine learning models can be trained to recognize when certain actions are appropriate based on predefined rules and the nature of the threat.

10.4.3 AI-Powered Threat Intelligence

AI/ML can enhance threat intelligence by analyzing large datasets from multiple sources, including threat intelligence feeds, network traffic data, and system logs. AI-driven systems can correlate information from these sources to identify new and emerging threats in real time. By automating the process of threat intelligence gathering and analysis, SOCs can stay ahead of cyber adversaries and reduce the time needed to detect and respond to new threats.

AI systems can also use predictive analytics to anticipate future attacks based on historical data and trends. For example, machine learning models can analyze previous cyberattacks on an organization and identify patterns that might suggest an impending threat. This predictive capability allows SOCs to take a proactive approach to cybersecurity, rather than merely reacting to incidents as they occur.

10.4.4 Case Study: AI-Enhanced SOC in a Financial Institution

A leading financial institution implemented AI-driven tools within its SOC to automate routine tasks and improve threat detection. The AI system analyzed incoming alerts, filtering out 80% of false positives and reducing the workload for human analysts. Additionally, the system used machine learning to detect previously unknown attack patterns, identifying threats 30% faster than the traditional SOC workflow. As a result, the institution saw a 25% reduction in response time for critical incidents, improving the overall security posture of the organization.

10.5 AI in Log Analysis and Threat Hunting: Automating Data Collection and Proactive Threat Detection

10.5.1 The Importance of Log Analysis in Cybersecurity

Log data is a critical component of cybersecurity, providing detailed records of system activity, user behavior, and network traffic. Analyzing these logs can reveal signs of cyberattacks, such as unauthorized access attempts, data exfiltration, or malware activity. However, the volume of log data generated by modern IT systems is immense, making manual analysis time-consuming and prone to human error. AI and ML can automate log analysis, enabling SOCs to quickly identify suspicious activity and respond to threats in real time.

10.5.2 AI-Driven Log Analysis

Machine learning algorithms can analyze log data in real time, identifying patterns and anomalies that may indicate a cyber threat. These algorithms can process large volumes of data more quickly and accurately than human analysts, reducing the time it takes to detect and respond to security incidents. Some key AI techniques used in log analysis include:

- **Pattern Recognition**: AI/ML systems can recognize normal patterns of system activity and flag deviations from these patterns as potential threats. For example, a machine learning model may detect unusual login times, unexpected spikes in data transfers, or abnormal access to sensitive files.
- **Anomaly Detection**: Unsupervised learning models can detect anomalies in log data without requiring labeled datasets. These models learn what constitutes "normal" behavior for a given system and flag any deviations for further investigation. Anomaly detection is particularly effective in identifying zero-day attacks or insider threats, where the behavior may not match known attack signatures.
- **Natural Language Processing (NLP) for Log Analysis**: NLP models can be used to analyze textual log data, such as system event messages or error reports. NLP can help SOC analysts quickly identify the most relevant information from large volumes of log entries, reducing the time spent manually reviewing logs.

10.5.3 Threat Hunting with AI and ML

Threat hunting is the proactive search for cyber threats that may have evaded detection by traditional security tools. AI and ML enhance threat hunting by automating the process of sifting through log data and identifying suspicious patterns. AI-driven threat hunting tools can analyze historical and real-time data to uncover hidden threats, enabling SOCs to neutralize attacks before they cause significant damage.

Machine learning models can continuously learn from new data, improving their ability to detect advanced threats over time. For example, AI-based threat hunting tools can detect lateral movement within a network, where attackers move between systems to escalate privileges or exfiltrate data. These tools can also identify indicators of compromise (IOCs) that may have been overlooked by traditional detection methods.

10.5.4 Case Study: AI in Threat Hunting

An e-commerce company faced an increasing number of cyberattacks targeting customer data and payment systems. The company's SOC implemented AI-driven threat hunting tools to analyze log data and network traffic. The AI system detected several instances of lateral movement within the network, where attackers had gained unauthorized access to internal systems. By identifying these threats early, the SOC was able to prevent a data breach and secure customer information. Over time, the AI system continued to improve its threat detection capabilities, reducing the time required for threat hunting by 40%.

10.6 Challenges in AI/ML Integration into SOCs

10.6.1 Technical Challenges

While AI and ML offer significant benefits to SOC operations, their integration is not without challenges. One of the primary technical challenges is the complexity of implementing AI/ML systems in a SOC environment. Developing, training, and fine-tuning machine learning models require access to large, high-quality datasets, which can be difficult to obtain.

■ **Data Quality and Availability**: AI/ML systems rely on high-quality data to function effectively. Poor-quality data, such as incomplete or mislabeled logs, can lead to inaccurate predictions and false positives. Organizations must ensure that their data collection processes are robust and that they have access to sufficient historical data for training machine learning models.

■ **Model Complexity and Scalability**: Machine learning models can be complex, requiring significant computational resources to train and deploy. As organizations scale their SOC operations, the infrastructure required to support AI-driven systems must also scale. This can be costly, particularly for organizations with limited IT budgets.

10.6.2 Ethical and Operational Challenges

In addition to technical challenges, there are ethical and operational considerations when integrating AI/ML into SOCs.

■ **Bias in AI Models**: AI models can inherit biases from the data they are trained on. For example, if a machine learning model is trained on data that overrepresents certain types of cyberattacks, it may be less effective at detecting other types of threats. SOCs must ensure that their AI/ML systems are trained on diverse datasets to avoid biased decision-making.

■ **Transparency and Explainability**: One of the challenges in using AI for threat detection is the "black box" nature of many machine learning models. These models can make accurate predictions, but it is often difficult to understand how they arrived at their conclusions. This lack of transparency can be problematic in SOC environments, where analysts need to explain their actions to stakeholders or regulators.

■ **Human-AI Collaboration**: AI is not a replacement for human analysts but rather a tool to augment their capabilities. Effective collaboration between AI systems and human SOC analysts is essential for successful operations. SOCs must strike a balance between automation and human oversight, ensuring that AI systems enhance, rather than replace, human decision-making.

10.6.3 AI and ML in Security and Data Privacy Concerns

The rapid advancement of Artificial Intelligence (AI) and Machine Learning (ML) technologies has revolutionized the field of cybersecurity, providing organizations with innovative capabilities to enhance their security protocols. However, the integration of AI and ML in cybersecurity also raises significant concerns regarding data privacy. Understanding these dynamics requires a thorough examination of the capabilities introduced by these technologies, as well as their implications for threat detection, response automation, and privacy issues.

10.6.3.1 Capabilities Introduced by AI and ML in Cybersecurity

AI and ML have ushered in a new era of advanced capabilities for cybersecurity, notably in the areas of threat intelligence, anomaly detection, and incident response.

1. **Threat Intelligence and Analysis**: AI technologies enable organizations to analyze vast volumes of data and extract relevant threat intelligence from diverse sources. Machine learning algorithms can identify trends and patterns within historical data, allowing cybersecurity teams to recognize emerging threats and attack vectors that could be detrimental to the organization (Baker et al., 2022). For instance, AI systems can aggregate information from security logs, network traffic, and external threat radar, providing a comprehensive situational awareness that manual analysis alone cannot achieve.

2. **Anomaly Detection**: ML algorithms excel in detecting anomalies within network traffic and user behavior, which are often indicative of potential threats. By establishing a baseline of normal activities, these algorithms can spot deviations that merit further investigation. A study by Ahmed et al. (2020) showcased the effectiveness of unsupervised learning models in identifying abnormal patterns, even in environments with high levels of legitimate user activity. This capability allows organizations to detect not just known threats but also novel attack methodologies that may otherwise go unnoticed by traditional detection methods.

3. **Automated Incident Response**: The automation of cybersecurity operations has been greatly enhanced through AI and ML technologies. Organizations can implement automated security frameworks that respond to incidents in real time, such as isolating affected systems or blocking malicious traffic without human intervention. For instance, AI systems can generate playbooks that dictate appropriate responses based on the behavior detected, significantly expediting the containment of security incidents (Shin et al., 2021). The ability to automate responses allows cybersecurity teams to focus on more strategic initiatives rather than being bogged down by routine incident handling.

10.6.3.2 Enabling Sophisticated Threat Detection and Response Mechanisms

The capabilities introduced by AI and ML substantially improve the sophistication of threat detection and response mechanisms in several ways:

1. **Improved Predictive Analytics**: Leveraging historical data, AI and ML algorithms can forecast potential threats and vulnerabilities before they materialize. Predictive analytics can assess risk levels by evaluating various factors, including asset sensitivity, user behavior trends, and previous attack patterns. Research conducted by Kaur et al. (2021) highlights the significant value of predictive analytics in preemptively identifying vulnerabilities, enabling organizations to mitigate risks before threats escalate into incidents.

2. **Contextual Awareness for Decision-Making**: AI-driven systems enhance incident response by providing contextual insights surrounding alerts and detections. By combining data from various sources, such as internal logs and external threat intelligence feeds, these systems can deliver a deeper situational understanding that informs response strategies. For example, an AI system can weigh the significance of an alert based on user roles, historical behavior, and the asset's critical nature, thereby helping analysts prioritize their efforts effectively (Stouffer et al., 2017).

3. **Continuous Learning and Adaptation**: AI and ML systems are inherently adaptive, allowing them to learn from past incidents and refine their detection capabilities. As they process new datasets, these systems update their algorithms to improve accuracy and responsiveness to emerging threats. Research by Duan et al. (2021) emphasizes how continuous learning frameworks significantly enhance the proficiency of AI in defense applications, enabling organizations to stay ahead of constantly evolving attack methods.

10.6.3.3 Data Privacy Concerns

While the capabilities of AI and ML enhance cybersecurity, they also raise significant data privacy concerns. The reliance on extensive datasets for training ML models can lead to unintended consequences for personal data protection. Issues surrounding the collection, processing, and usage of sensitive information must be addressed to ensure compliance with regulations such as the General Data Protection Regulation (GDPR) and the California Consumer Privacy Act (CCPA).

A study by Linn et al. (2020) identified the main organizational barriers to implementing responsible AI practices, finding that a lack of specialized tools for tracking data provenance was a significant hurdle to ensuring transparency. Moreover, ethical considerations must guide the development and deployment of AI systems, emphasizing the need for fairness, accountability, and transparency in algorithms, which may inherently introduce bias or discrimination if not meticulously designed.

This chapter explores the primary security and privacy risks associated with AI/ML systems, discusses the implications of these technologies for data protection laws, and provides guidance on mitigating these risks while adhering to compliance standards.

10.6.4 Adversarial Attacks on AI Systems

One of the most prominent security risks in AI/ML systems is adversarial attacks, where malicious actors intentionally manipulate inputs to deceive machine learning models. These attacks exploit vulnerabilities in the way AI systems process data, often leading to incorrect outputs that could have severe consequences in security-critical applications.

- **Adversarial Examples**: Attackers can craft input data, known as adversarial examples, that are designed to appear normal to humans but cause AI systems to make incorrect classifications or predictions. For instance, a seemingly benign image can be subtly altered to fool an AI-based facial recognition system into misidentifying a person. In the context of cybersecurity, adversarial examples can trick AI models into misclassifying malware as legitimate software, leading to undetected breaches.
- **Model Poisoning**: Model poisoning attacks occur when an attacker manipulates the training data used to build an AI model, introducing corrupted data that causes the model to make incorrect decisions in future predictions. Poisoning attacks can have devastating effects in environments where AI is used to detect threats, such as Security Operations Centers (SOCs). By altering the model's understanding of what constitutes a threat, attackers can evade detection and gain unauthorized access to systems.
- **Defense Strategies**: Organizations must adopt defense mechanisms to protect AI systems from adversarial attacks. Techniques such

as adversarial training—where models are trained on both normal and adversarial inputs—can increase the robustness of AI systems. Additionally, anomaly detection systems can be used to monitor AI behavior and flag unusual activity that might indicate an adversarial attack.

10.6.5 Data Poisoning and Integrity Risks

Data is the foundation of AI/ML models, and the security of this data is paramount to the success of AI-driven cybersecurity initiatives. Data poisoning, as mentioned earlier, is a significant threat that can affect the integrity of training datasets, leading to biased or inaccurate models.

- **Impact on Model Performance**: Poisoned datasets can degrade the performance of AI models, leading to misclassification or failure to detect anomalies. For example, if an attacker injects incorrect labels into a training dataset used for malware detection, the resulting model may struggle to identify actual malware, exposing the system to risk.
- **Mitigation Techniques**: To mitigate data poisoning risks, organizations should implement robust data validation processes, ensuring that the data used to train AI models is accurate and reliable. Additionally, techniques such as differential privacy and secure multiparty computation can be used to protect the integrity of training data while maintaining privacy.

10.6.6 Model Theft and Reverse Engineering

AI models, especially those used in high-stakes security applications, are valuable intellectual property. Model theft or reverse engineering is a growing concern, where attackers attempt to replicate proprietary AI models by either extracting them through API access or using techniques to deduce the model's architecture and parameters.

- **Implications of Model Theft**: If an attacker can steal or replicate a security-critical AI model, they may gain the ability to predict its behavior, allowing them to evade detection or develop strategies to exploit the model's weaknesses. This is particularly concerning in industries like finance or healthcare, where AI models are used to protect sensitive data.

- **Preventive Measures**: To protect AI models from theft, organizations should implement API rate limiting, require authentication for model access, and use techniques such as model watermarking to track intellectual property. Additionally, cryptographic techniques like homomorphic encryption can help secure AI models, even when they are deployed in untrusted environments.

10.7 Data Privacy Concerns in AI/ML

10.7.1 AI and Privacy Regulations: GDPR and CCPA

With AI models increasingly relying on vast amounts of data, the intersection of AI/ML and data privacy has become a significant area of concern, especially with regulations such as the General Data Protection Regulation (GDPR) in Europe and the California Consumer Privacy Act (CCPA) in the United States.

- **Data Minimization**: Under GDPR, organizations are required to adhere to the principle of data minimization, collecting only the data necessary for specific purposes. AI models, which thrive on large datasets, can easily conflict with this requirement if not carefully managed. Organizations must ensure that their AI systems are designed to collect and process only the data necessary for their intended functions.
- **Right to Explanation**: GDPR also includes provisions for the "right to explanation," which gives individuals the right to understand how decisions that affect them are made by automated systems. AI/ML models, particularly those built using deep learning, are often seen as "black boxes" with limited transparency. This can pose compliance challenges, as organizations may struggle to provide clear explanations for decisions made by AI models.
- **Mitigating Privacy Risks**: To mitigate privacy risks, organizations can employ techniques such as data anonymization, which removes personally identifiable information (PII) from datasets. Differential privacy, a mathematical technique that adds noise to data to prevent the identification of individuals, is also gaining traction to protect privacy while still allowing AI models to learn from large datasets.

10.7.2 Data Breaches and AI Systems

AI systems themselves can be a target of data breaches, especially since they often store or process large volumes of sensitive information. A data breach in an AI system can lead to the exposure of both the training data and the model's internal parameters, potentially causing significant reputational and financial harm.

■ **Breaches in AI Models**: AI models that process sensitive personal or financial data—such as those used in healthcare, finance, or government—are particularly vulnerable. A breach in an AI system can lead to the exposure of PII, trade secrets, or other confidential information. Organizations must treat AI models and the data they process with the same level of security as any other critical IT system.

■ **AI as a Breach Vector**: AI models themselves can be used as vectors for data breaches. For example, an attacker could manipulate input data to extract sensitive information about the training dataset—a technique known as model inversion. This poses a significant privacy risk, particularly when AI models are trained on sensitive or proprietary data.

10.7.3 Ethics and AI: Bias and Fairness

In addition to privacy concerns, ethical issues related to bias and fairness are increasingly coming to the forefront as AI models become more prevalent in decision-making processes. AI systems trained on biased datasets can perpetuate or even exacerbate existing societal biases, leading to unfair outcomes.

■ **Bias in AI Models**: AI systems are only as good as the data they are trained on. If the training data reflects biases—whether based on race, gender, or socioeconomic status—these biases can be encoded into the model itself. For example, AI models used in financial services for credit scoring have been shown to exhibit racial and gender biases, leading to unfair lending practices.

■ **Ensuring Fairness and Accountability**: To address these concerns, organizations must carefully audit their AI models to identify and mitigate bias. Techniques such as fairness-aware machine learning, where models are trained to minimize bias while maintaining accuracy, are increasingly being adopted. Moreover, organizations must ensure that they have processes in place to audit and update AI models as societal norms and legal requirements evolve.

10.7.4 Case Study: AI and Privacy in Healthcare

The healthcare sector is one of the most data-intensive industries, with AI systems playing an increasingly important role in diagnosis, treatment recommendations, and patient care. However, the sensitive nature of health data, combined with stringent privacy regulations such as HIPAA (Health Insurance Portability and Accountability Act) in the United States, poses significant challenges for the deployment of AI in healthcare.

- **Privacy Risks**: AI systems in healthcare often require access to large volumes of patient data to deliver accurate results. This raises privacy concerns, as data breaches or misuse of patient information can have severe consequences for both patients and healthcare providers. Additionally, healthcare AI systems must comply with HIPAA, which mandates strict controls on the storage, transmission, and processing of patient data.
- **Privacy-Preserving AI**: To address these challenges, healthcare organizations are increasingly turning to privacy-preserving AI techniques. Federated learning, for example, allows AI models to be trained on decentralized data without sharing raw patient information across organizations. This approach can help protect patient privacy while still enabling AI models to learn from large datasets.

10.8 Mitigating AI and ML Security and Privacy Risks

10.8.1 Privacy-Preserving Machine Learning

As privacy regulations become more stringent, privacy-preserving machine learning (PPML) techniques have emerged to reconcile the need for large datasets with the requirement to protect individual privacy. PPML uses a combination of cryptographic techniques, data anonymization, and decentralized learning to enable AI models to learn from data without compromising privacy.

- **Federated Learning**: Federated learning is a technique that allows AI models to be trained on decentralized data, meaning that raw data never leaves the local device or system. Instead, only model updates are shared, preserving the privacy of individual data points. This approach is particularly useful in industries like healthcare and finance, where data privacy is paramount.
- **Differential Privacy**: Differential privacy is a mathematical framework that adds noise to datasets to prevent the identification of individual data points. By ensuring that individual contributions to a dataset are indistinguishable within the aggregate output, differential privacy provides a robust, quantifiable guarantee of individual privacy. This allows organizations to safely use and share aggregated data for training AI models without compromising the confidentiality of the people represented in the data.

Chapter 11

Ethical Considerations and Risks of AI/ML in Cybersecurity

As Artificial Intelligence (AI) and Machine Learning (ML) become central to cybersecurity protocols, the ethical implications and risks associated with these technologies require careful examination. While AI and ML offer immense potential to enhance cybersecurity, their deployment also raises concerns about fairness, transparency, accountability, and the risk of misuse.

The integration of Artificial Intelligence (AI) and Machine Learning (ML) into cybersecurity is revolutionizing the landscape of threat detection and response. However, the deployment of these powerful technologies also carries significant ethical considerations and risks that must be thoroughly examined. From issues of fairness and transparency to accountability and potential misuse, understanding the ethical implications is crucial for safe and responsible implementation.

11.1 Ethical Implications and Risks of AI/ ML in Cybersecurity

1. **Bias and Discrimination**: One of the major ethical concerns surrounding AI and ML is the potential for bias in algorithmic decision-making. If the training data used to develop AI models include inherent biases, these biases can propagate into the decision-making processes

of AI systems. For example, an AI-driven cybersecurity system trained on data featuring a predominance of certain user profiles may unfairly target or neglect other groups, leading to disparities in threat responses. Research by Mehrabi et al. (2019) highlights how biased datasets can cause discriminatory outcomes that may unjustly affect individuals based on race, gender, or socioeconomic status.

2. **Privacy Risks**: The use of AI and ML in cybersecurity often necessitates the analysis of large datasets, which may include personal or sensitive information. Such data utilization can pose significant privacy concerns, particularly if data is collected without user consent. Regulations like the General Data Protection Regulation (GDPR) outline strict guidelines for data handling and emphasize the need for explicit consent. Failure to comply with these regulations can lead to severe consequences for organizations and adversely affect consumers (Voigt & Von dem Bussche, 2017).

3. **Lack of Transparency**: Many AI models act as "black boxes," where organizations may struggle to understand how decisions are made by algorithms. This lack of transparency can undermine trust and accountability. In cybersecurity, where the stakes are high, users and stakeholders should understand and trust the rationale behind detection and response actions taken by AI systems. Research has shown that SOC analysts are more likely to act on AI-generated alerts if the system provides a clear explanation for its reasoning (Arrieta et al., 2020).

4. **Potential for Misuse**: The capabilities of AI and ML could be exploited by malicious actors to conduct cyberattacks with greater precision and efficiency. For instance, techniques associated with AI can be used to create deepfake videos or automate spear-phishing campaigns (Scully, 2021). Responsible governance is needed to ensure that these technologies do not enable adversaries but rather secure and protect systems.

11.2 Regulations for Responsible Use of AI and ML

To ensure that AI and ML are used responsibly in cybersecurity, it is vital to develop robust regulatory frameworks. Existing regulations can serve as models, while additional guidelines may need to be crafted to address the unique challenges posed by these technologies.

1. **Accountability Frameworks**: Organizations implementing AI and ML should be held accountable for their outcomes. This includes ensuring that organizations handle data ethically and transparently, as well as putting mechanisms in place to address mistakes and failures in AI systems (Binns, 2018). Developing an accountability framework that emphasizes corporate responsibility and oversight when deploying these technologies is critical.

2. **Data Transparency Regulations**: Regulations similar to GDPR's Article 22 could mandate transparency for AI decision-making. Organizations should disclose when AI systems are involved in decision processes and provide users with an explanation of how their data is used. In line with this, enforceable guidelines that require AI models to be interpretable will empower users to understand the basis for decisions made regarding security (Burrell, 2016).

3. **Ethical AI Guidelines**: Regulatory bodies should create and enforce ethical AI guidelines for cybersecurity, including protocols for data quality and fairness. The feasibility of this is supported by research; Jobin et al. (2019) demonstrated that a global consensus on these core principles already exists, providing a clear template for action.

11.3 Guardrails against Misuse of AI and ML

As AI and ML technologies evolve, introducing specific guardrails can help mitigate the risks of misuse while emphasizing ethical considerations:

1. **Robust Testing Protocols**: Before deploying AI systems, comprehensive testing should validate their reliability, accuracy, and fairness. Regular audits, performance metrics, and assessments of training data can help identify and rectify biases, ensuring that the algorithms operate as intended without unintended consequences (Leitner & Stiefmueller, 2019).

2. **Stakeholder Engagement**: A 2021 case study by Kaye et al. demonstrated the value of stakeholder engagement by documenting how feedback from patient advocacy groups led to critical changes in a clinical AI tool, improving its fairness and aligning it with community ethical standards.

3. **Ethical AI Committees**: Organizations can establish committees tasked with the ethical oversight of AI/ML implementations. These committees would be responsible for ensuring that AI technologies used in cybersecurity adhere to ethical guidelines, privacy standards, and the principles of fairness and accountability.

This chapter also explores key areas: Bias in AI/ML algorithms, the potential for cybercriminals to exploit AI/ML for malicious purposes, and the ethical deployment of AI in cybersecurity operations.

11.4 Bias in AI/ML Algorithms: Addressing Algorithmic Bias and Fairness in Cybersecurity Applications

11.4.1 Understanding Bias in AI/ML Systems

AI/ML systems are only as unbiased as the data and algorithms used to build them. Bias in AI refers to the presence of systematic errors that disproportionately affect certain groups or outcomes. In the context of cybersecurity, biased AI models can result in unfair or discriminatory decisions, such as disproportionately flagging activities from certain demographics or falsely identifying benign behavior as malicious.

- **Sources of Bias**: Bias can be introduced into AI/ML systems at various stages, including during data collection, feature selection, and model training. For example, if a dataset used to train an AI system contains overrepresentations of certain types of attacks or behaviors, the model may become biased toward detecting those specific scenarios while overlooking others.
- **Impact on Cybersecurity**: In cybersecurity, bias can manifest in several ways. A biased AI system might unfairly target certain users or geographic regions, resulting in over-policing in some areas while leaving other vulnerabilities exposed. Furthermore, biased models might fail to detect certain types of cyberattacks if those attacks are underrepresented in the training data. This lack of inclusivity can lead to blind spots in an organization's security posture.

11.4.2 Case Study: Bias in Threat Detection Systems

A well-documented example of bias in AI systems can be found in facial recognition technology. In 2019, studies showed that facial recognition systems had significantly higher error rates for identifying individuals with darker skin tones compared to lighter-skinned individuals. This type of bias can similarly occur in cybersecurity applications, particularly in threat detection systems that rely on user behavior analytics.

For example, a banking institution implemented an AI-based fraud detection system designed to flag suspicious activities based on transaction patterns. However, the system disproportionately flagged transactions from individuals in certain regions due to a biased dataset that overrepresented fraud in those areas. This led to an increase in false positives and complaints of discrimination. The bank was forced to retrain the model using a more representative dataset, improving its fairness and reducing bias.

11.4.3 Addressing Bias in Cybersecurity AI Systems

Mitigating bias in AI/ML systems requires a multifaceted approach that focuses on data collection, model training, and ongoing monitoring. Some strategies include:

- **Diverse and Representative Datasets**: Ensuring that the data used to train AI models is diverse and representative of the entire population is key to reducing bias. In cybersecurity, this means incorporating data from a wide range of attack vectors, user behaviors, and geographic regions.
- **Bias Audits**: Regular bias audits should be conducted to assess whether an AI system is producing biased outcomes. These audits can help identify discrepancies in how different groups or scenarios are treated by the model.
- **Fairness-Aware Algorithms**: Incorporating fairness-aware algorithms into the development process can help reduce bias. These algorithms are designed to minimize disparate impacts on different groups by adjusting how the model treats certain features or outcomes.
- **Human Oversight**: Human-in-the-loop (HITL) approaches ensure that AI decisions are reviewed by human analysts, particularly in high-stakes scenarios. This oversight can help catch biased outcomes and provide an additional layer of accountability.

11.5 AI in the Hands of Cybercriminals: How Adversaries Can Leverage AI and ML for Malicious Purposes

11.5.1 AI as a Double-Edged Sword

The rapid advancement and integration of Artificial Intelligence (AI) and Machine Learning (ML) into cybersecurity have the potential to significantly enhance organizational defenses against an ever-evolving threat landscape. However, these same technologies can also be repurposed by cybercriminals, creating a perilous duality where AI serves both as a shield and as a sword. Understanding this dichotomy is crucial for organizations striving to protect themselves while acknowledging the tools that adversaries may deploy.

11.5.1.1 Adoption of AI and ML by Cybercriminals

Cybercriminals have increasingly recognized the benefits of AI and ML, adapting these technologies to enhance their malicious capabilities. Historically, cyberattacks required significant manual effort and technical expertise. However, as AI technologies have become more accessible, even less sophisticated actors can leverage these tools, thus democratizing the ability to commit cybercrime (Bertino & Islam, 2019).

Recent studies illustrate various ways in which AI and ML are being co-opted by cybercriminals. One significant area is in the realm of phishing attacks. Cybercriminals utilize AI to create tailored phishing emails that mimic legitimate communications more convincingly. By analyzing language patterns and user behavior on social media, adversaries can craft messages that are more likely to deceive targets (Aryan et al., 2021). This level of personalization increases the likelihood of successful attacks, making traditional detection methods less effective.

In response to AI-generated polymorphic malware, Sanz et al. (2020) proposed a deep learning-based detection system that analyzes behavioral patterns instead of static signatures, effectively identifying malicious code that continually changes its characteristics. With evidence mounting that Ransomware-as-a-Service (RaaS) models are using AI to optimize attacks, the cyber threat landscape is evolving rapidly. Academics like Wright (2021) have begun to analyze the profound implications of this trend, warning that it could lead to an increase in the scale and frequency of devastating operations.

11.5.1.2 *Automating and Scaling Cyberattacks*

The scalability that AI provides to cybercriminals is transformative. By automating aspects of cyberattacks, adversaries can launch more attacks in less time, increasing both the frequency and volume of malicious activities. For example, AI-driven bots can conduct reconnaissance on thousands of potential targets in a matter of minutes, gathering critical information and identifying vulnerabilities faster than human attackers ever could (Priyadarshini, Kumar, Tuan, Son, Long, Sharma, & Rai, 2021).

Furthermore, AI systems can enhance the effectiveness of Distributed Denial-of-Service (DDoS) attacks. By analyzing network traffic patterns, criminals can use AI to identify the most effective approach for overwhelming targets, adjusting their tactics in real time based on the defensive measures activated by the victim (Yampolskiy, 2018).

In the realm of data breaches, AI can help cybercriminals optimize their approaches for exploiting vulnerabilities. Machine learning algorithms can analyze past data breaches, identifying patterns and common entry points that successful attacks have taken. This information enables adversaries to target their efforts strategically, maximizing the chances of infiltration. According to research by Katiyar, Tripathi, Kumar, Verma, Sahu, and Saxena (2024), AI can actively assist in identifying and exploiting "zero-day" vulnerabilities— those that are unknown to software vendors and security professionals. This capacity represents an alarming escalation in the cyber threat landscape.

Moreover, the use of AI in social engineering tactics is a growing concern. By utilizing chatbots and other conversational AI tools, cybercriminals can engage potential victims in realistic interactions, further increasing their likelihood of success in scams (Peisert et al., 2020). This capability highlights the importance of enhancing public awareness around social engineering and providing training to recognize and mitigate such attacks.

While AI and ML have the potential to revolutionize cybersecurity defenses, these technologies are also being adopted by cybercriminals to enhance their malicious capabilities. AI can be used by adversaries to automate and scale cyberattacks, evade detection, and exploit vulnerabilities more effectively. This dual-use nature of AI raises significant concerns about the evolving threat landscape.

■ **AI-Driven Phishing Attacks**: AI can be used to generate highly sophisticated phishing emails that are tailored to individual targets. By analyzing large amounts of data about a person's online behavior, social media activity, and communication style, AI can craft personalized messages that are more likely to deceive the recipient. AI-generated phishing campaigns can also scale rapidly, targeting thousands of individuals simultaneously with minimal human intervention.

■ **AI in Malware Development**: AI-powered malware can adapt to its environment in real time, making it more difficult for traditional security systems to detect and respond. For example, AI-based malware can learn from the defenses it encounters, altering its behavior to avoid detection by antivirus software or intrusion detection systems. This type of malware can also use ML algorithms to identify vulnerable systems and prioritize targets based on their security posture.

■ **Automated Social Engineering**: AI can enhance social engineering attacks by automating the process of gathering and analyzing information about potential victims. AI-driven systems can analyze public data, such as social media profiles, to identify vulnerabilities in human behavior that can be exploited. This allows cybercriminals to create highly convincing social engineering attacks with minimal effort.

11.5.2 Case Study: AI-Powered Ransomware

In 2021, a new strain of AI-powered ransomware, dubbed "DeepLocker," demonstrated the potential for AI-enhanced cyberattacks. DeepLocker used deep learning algorithms to hide its malicious payload within legitimate applications, only activating the ransomware when specific conditions were met, such as the presence of a particular individual's face or voice. This highly targeted approach made DeepLocker more difficult to detect and allowed it to evade traditional security mechanisms.

This case highlights the growing sophistication of AI-driven attacks and the need for advanced security measures to counter them. As AI-powered cyberattacks become more prevalent, organizations must adapt their defenses to anticipate and neutralize these evolving threats.

11.5.3 Defense against AI-Driven Cybercrime

To defend against AI-driven cybercrime, organizations must leverage the same technologies to enhance their cybersecurity defenses. Some strategies include:

- **AI-Powered Threat Detection**: AI and ML can be used to detect and mitigate AI-driven attacks by analyzing network traffic, user behaviors, and system logs in real time. These systems can identify anomalies and patterns that indicate malicious activity, even when the attack is highly sophisticated or adaptive.
- **Adversarial AI Research**: Organizations should invest in adversarial AI research to understand how AI systems can be manipulated by attackers. By identifying potential vulnerabilities in AI models, cybersecurity teams can develop more robust defenses against AI-driven threats.
- **Collaboration and Information Sharing**: The cybersecurity community must collaborate to share information about emerging AI-driven threats. Threat intelligence sharing between organizations, governments, and cybersecurity vendors is critical to staying ahead of cybercriminals who leverage AI.

11.6 Ethical AI Deployment: Best Practices for Responsible AI Use in Cybersecurity

11.6.1 Privacy and Data Protection in AI Systems

The deployment of AI in cybersecurity often involves the processing of large volumes of data, including sensitive personal information. Ensuring privacy and data protection is a critical ethical consideration when deploying AI systems.

- **Data Minimization**: Organizations should adopt data minimization principles, collecting only the data necessary for AI-driven cybersecurity systems to function effectively. Over-collection of data can increase the risk of data breaches and privacy violations.
- **Data Anonymization**: To protect the privacy of individuals, organizations should anonymize data used for training AI models. This involves removing personally identifiable information (PII) from datasets to ensure that individuals cannot be identified, even if the data is compromised.
- **Compliance with Regulations**: AI systems must be designed to comply with data protection regulations such as the General Data Protection Regulation (GDPR) and the California Consumer Privacy Act (CCPA).

These regulations impose strict requirements on how personal data can be collected, processed, and stored, and organizations must ensure that their AI systems adhere to these standards.

11.6.2 Transparency and Explainability

AI systems, particularly those used in cybersecurity, must be transparent and explainable. One of the common criticisms of AI is that many models, particularly deep learning models, operate as "black boxes," making it difficult to understand how decisions are made.

- **Explainable AI (XAI)**: Explainable AI refers to AI systems that provide insights into how decisions are made. In cybersecurity, this is critical for ensuring accountability and trust. For example, if an AI system flags a particular user's behavior as malicious, security analysts must be able to understand why the AI made that decision in order to take appropriate action.
- **Accountability in AI-Driven Decisions**: Organizations must establish clear accountability for decisions made by AI systems. This includes identifying who is responsible for reviewing AI decisions and ensuring that those decisions align with the organization's security policies and ethical standards.

11.6.3 Human-AI Collaboration

While AI has the potential to automate many aspects of cybersecurity, human oversight remains essential. AI should be viewed as a tool to augment human decision-making, not replace it.

- **Human-in-the-Loop (HITL) Systems**: HITL systems ensure that human analysts are involved in critical decision-making processes, particularly when AI systems make high-stakes or ambiguous decisions. This collaborative approach combines the efficiency of AI with the intuition and expertise of human analysts.
- **Continuous Monitoring and Evaluation**: AI systems should be continuously monitored and evaluated to ensure that they are functioning as intended.

Chapter 12

Conclusion: Leveraging Artificial Intelligence and Machine Learning to Improve Cybersecurity Protocols

As we conclude this exploration into the transformative potential of Artificial Intelligence (AI) and Machine Learning (ML) in cybersecurity, we have witnessed the profound impact these technologies can have on enhancing cybersecurity protocols. This book has covered a wide spectrum of topics, from the foundational principles of AI and ML to their practical applications in threat detection, data privacy, fraud prevention, and Security Operations Centers. By integrating these advanced technologies into their frameworks, organizations can not only bolster their defenses but also adopt a proactive stance against the increasingly sophisticated nexus of cyber threats.

The work laid out in this book provides valuable insights into the multifaceted role of AI and ML technologies in the contemporary cybersecurity landscape. We have established that the complexities of modern cyber threats necessitate a departure from traditional security measures that rely on static methods of protection. AI and ML enhance the capabilities of cybersecurity professionals by enabling them to automate responses, detect anomalies in real time, and leverage predictive analytics to anticipate potential attacks. Moreover, AI-driven systems can significantly improve the efficiency and effectiveness of Security Operations Centers (SOCs) through continuous monitoring and adaptive learning.

DOI: 10.4324/9781003615026-12

12.1 Leveraging the Book for Diverse Audiences

The knowledge captured in this book is intended to serve a broad audience, including students, cybersecurity professionals, and leaders in the C-suite.

For Students: This book can be a foundational resource for those studying cybersecurity, providing a comprehensive understanding of how AI and ML technologies shape the future of the field. Students are encouraged to leverage the case studies and practical examples to bridge the gap between theory and practice. Engaging deeply with the content can foster skills that are increasingly sought after in the job market, positioning students as innovative problem-solvers capable of navigating the challenges posed by emerging technologies.

For Cybersecurity Professionals: Industry practitioners can utilize the insights discussed here to enhance their existing security frameworks. By employing the techniques for threat detection, data privacy management, and incident response outlined in this book, cybersecurity professionals can improve their organizations' security postures. Moreover, the book emphasizes the importance of ethical considerations and responsible AI usage, equipping professionals with the knowledge they need to implement best practices in AI and ML deployment.

For Leadership (C-Suite): Decision-makers in organizations will benefit from the discussions on the strategic value that AI and ML bring to cybersecurity. By understanding the operational advantages and the potential return on investment that these technologies deliver, C-suite leaders can champion initiatives to adopt and integrate AI-driven solutions within their organizations. The book provides frameworks to align cybersecurity investments with overall business objectives, emphasizing a culture of security that incorporates advanced technologies.

12.2 Proposed Future Research Directions

While this book provides a robust foundation for understanding the intersection of AI, ML, and cybersecurity, further research is essential to address the nuances of responsible AI use in this fast-evolving domain. Some key areas for future research include:

1. **Ethical AI Practices**: Continued exploration into ethical considerations associated with AI and ML in cybersecurity is critical. Research should focus on establishing frameworks that emphasize fairness,

accountability, and transparency in AI algorithms, ensuring that their deployment minimizes biases and safeguards user privacy.

2. **Regulatory Compliance**: Investigating the evolving regulatory landscape concerning AI and data privacy is crucial. This includes examining how existing regulations can adapt to accommodate the unique challenges posed by AI tools and how organizations can align their practices with legal frameworks and standards.

3. **Long-Term Effects on the Workforce**: The integration of AI and ML in cybersecurity could lead to shifts in workforce dynamics. Research must address how adopting these technologies impacts the nature of cybersecurity roles, workforce training, and the necessary skillsets for future professionals in the field.

4. **Advanced Threat Landscape Analysis**: As adversaries adopt AI and ML to enhance their malicious capabilities, it is vital to conduct ongoing research into the effectiveness of AI systems in detecting and mitigating advanced cyber threats, including APTs and zero-day vulnerabilities.

In summary, "Leveraging Artificial Intelligence and Machine Learning to Improve Cybersecurity Protocols" serves as a crucial resource for understanding the potential and challenges of integrating AI and ML into cybersecurity practices. By equipping students, professionals, and leadership with the knowledge to navigate this evolving landscape, we can strive toward a more secure digital future, leveraging the innovations these technologies offer while remaining vigilant about the ethical implications of their use.

Appendices

A.1 Leveraging Artificial Intelligence (AI) and Machine Learning to Improve Cybersecurity Protocols

This appendix section provides critical resources, terms, tools, and references necessary to fully understand and implement AI and ML technologies in cybersecurity environments. The glossary clarifies technical terms, while the list of tools showcases industry-leading platforms available to practitioners. The references and further reading offer in-depth knowledge to further explore the intersection of AI, ML, and cybersecurity.

A.2 Glossary of Terms

- **Adversarial Attack**: A type of attack where malicious actors manipulate AI/ML inputs (such as images or data) to deceive the system and cause it to make incorrect predictions or classifications.
- **Advanced Persistent Threat (APT)**: A prolonged and targeted cyberattack in which an unauthorized user gains access to a network and remains undetected for an extended period.
- **Artificial Intelligence (AI)**: The simulation of human intelligence by machines, especially computer systems, which includes processes such as learning (acquiring information and rules), reasoning (using rules to reach conclusions), and self-correction.
- **Behavioral Analytics**: The process of analyzing patterns in human or system behavior to detect abnormal actions that could indicate a cybersecurity threat.

- **Bias (in AI)**: The systematic and unfair discrimination in AI systems, often resulting from biased data used to train the models, leading to skewed or inaccurate outcomes.
- **Black Box Model**: A term used to describe AI models whose internal workings are not easily understood or interpretable, often making it difficult to understand how decisions are made.
- **Data Poisoning**: A type of attack where malicious actors tamper with the training data used in machine learning models to degrade the performance or cause the model to make incorrect predictions.
- **Deep Learning**: A subset of machine learning that uses neural networks with many layers (deep networks) to model complex patterns and relationships in data.
- **Differential Privacy**: A method of ensuring that the release of data and results from AI/ML models does not compromise the privacy of individuals whose data is used in training.
- **Explainable AI (XAI)**: AI systems that are designed to be transparent, providing clear and understandable reasons for their decisions and actions.
- **Federated Learning**: A privacy-preserving machine learning technique that allows AI models to be trained across decentralized data sources without exchanging raw data.
- **False Positive**: An incorrect result in which benign activity is mistakenly identified as malicious by a cybersecurity system or model.
- **Generative Adversarial Networks (GANs)**: A class of machine learning frameworks where two neural networks contest with each other (a generator and a discriminator) to produce new data instances that can resemble real data.
- **Intrusion Detection System (IDS)**: A system that monitors network traffic for suspicious activities and issues alerts when potential intrusions are detected.
- **Lateral Movement**: A technique used by attackers to move across a network after gaining initial access, allowing them to search for sensitive data and escalate their privileges.
- **Machine Learning (ML)**: A branch of AI that focuses on the development of algorithms that can learn from and make decisions based on data.
- **Natural Language Processing (NLP)**: A field of AI that focuses on the interaction between computers and humans through natural language, often used in analyzing text for security purposes, such as identifying phishing emails.

- **Phishing**: A form of cyberattack where attackers deceive individuals into disclosing sensitive information by posing as legitimate entities.
- **Security Operations Center (SOC)**: A centralized unit within an organization responsible for monitoring, detecting, responding to, and mitigating cybersecurity incidents.
- **Supervised Learning**: A type of machine learning where a model is trained on labeled data, meaning the correct output is provided for each input during the training phase.
- **Unsupervised Learning**: A type of machine learning where a model is trained on data without labeled outcomes, meaning it must find patterns and relationships on its own.
- **Zero-Day Exploit**: A software vulnerability that is unknown to the software vendor and has not been patched, leaving systems exposed to attack until a solution is developed.

List of AI/ML Tools and Platforms for Cybersecurity

1. **Darktrace**: A leading AI-powered cybersecurity platform that uses machine learning to detect and respond to cyber threats in real time by analyzing network traffic and user behavior.
2. **Cortex XDR (Palo Alto Networks)**: A platform that integrates AI and machine learning to provide advanced endpoint detection and response, network traffic analysis, and threat intelligence.
3. **IBM QRadar**: A security intelligence platform that uses AI to analyze log data, network traffic, and threat intelligence to detect and respond to security threats in real time.
4. **Splunk**: A platform for real-time analysis of machine data, which incorporates AI and machine learning for detecting anomalies and predicting potential security incidents.
5. **Vectra AI**: A platform that uses AI-driven network detection and response (NDR) to identify and mitigate cyberattacks through continuous monitoring of network traffic.
6. **Symantec Endpoint Protection (SEP)**: A security platform that incorporates AI and ML to provide real-time protection against malware, ransomware, and other advanced threats.
7. **Microsoft Azure Sentinel**: A cloud-native SIEM platform that uses machine learning and AI to provide threat detection, incident response, and automation for security operations.

8. **Elastic Security (Elastic Stack)**: A platform that integrates AI-driven analytics for SIEM, providing threat detection, prevention, and response through comprehensive log data analysis.

9. **CylancePROTECT (BlackBerry)**: A machine learning-driven endpoint protection platform that uses AI to predict, prevent, detect, and respond to threats.

10. **FireEye Helix**: A security operations platform that integrates AI and machine learning to enhance SOC capabilities, automate workflows, and improve threat detection and response.

11. **AWS GuardDuty**: An AI-powered threat detection service that uses machine learning to continuously monitor AWS accounts for malicious or unauthorized behavior.

12. **Google Cloud Security Command Center (SCC)**: A comprehensive security and risk management platform that integrates machine learning to identify and mitigate security risks in Google Cloud environments.

13. **Deep Instinct**: A deep learning-based cybersecurity platform that provides real-time prevention, detection, and response to known and unknown malware threats.

14. **Sift Science**: A platform that uses machine learning to detect and prevent online fraud by analyzing user behavior and transaction data for signs of fraudulent activity.

15. **RSA NetWitness**: A threat detection and response platform that leverages machine learning to analyze logs, network traffic, and endpoint data for faster threat detection and incident response.

16. **FortiAI (Fortinet)**: A cybersecurity solution that uses deep learning to automate malware analysis, improve threat detection, and reduce response times in SOC environments.

17. **Rapid7 InsightIDR**: A cloud-based platform that integrates machine learning to detect and respond to cyber threats by analyzing user behavior and security event data.

18. **Exabeam**: A platform for user and entity behavior analytics (UEBA) that uses machine learning to detect insider threats and external attacks by analyzing user behavior patterns.

19. **Tanium**: A cybersecurity platform that integrates machine learning to provide endpoint security, continuous monitoring, and real-time visibility into IT assets.

References

Abdalla, H. S., & Ahmed, S. (2021). The role of machine learning in cybersecurity risk management. *International Journal of Information Security, 20*(3), 351–372.

Aborisade, A., Agbaje, A., & Elisha, B. (2020). Building the next generation cybersecurity workforce: How training programs can make a difference. *Journal of Cybersecurity Education, Research and Practice, 2020*(1).

Ahmad, A., Maynard, S. B., & Park, S. (2014). Information security strategies: Towards an organizational multi-strategy perspective. *Journal of Intelligent Manufacturing, 25*(2), 357–370.

Ahmed, M., Mahmood, A. N., & Hu, J. (2020). A survey of network anomaly detection techniques. *Journal of Network and Computer Applications, 115*, 1–30.

Alazab, M., et al. (2020). Security analytics: A study on the state of the art and future directions. *IEEE Access, 8*, 28554–28568.

Alcaraz, C., & Zeadally, S. (2020). Cybersecurity for critical infrastructures: A survey. *Journal of Network and Computer Applications, 188*, 103140.

Alcaraz, C., & Zeadally, S. (2021). Cybersecurity for critical infrastructures: A survey. *Journal of Network and Computer Applications, 188*, 103140.

Ajmal, M., Khan, S., & Lee, J. (2021). A Dynamic Thresholding Framework for Network Anomaly Detection Using Adaptive Machine Learning. *Journal of Network and Systems Management, 29*(3), 45. https://doi.org/10.1007/s10922-021-09608-6

Anderson, R., Cheshin, A., & Kovalchik, A. (2020). The cybersecurity skills gap: A focus on the workforce. *International Journal of Information Security, 19*(4), 331–344.

Arrieta, A. B., Díaz-Rodríguez, N., Del Ser, J., Bennetot, A., Tabik, S., Barbado, A., ... & Herrera, F. (2020). Explainable Artificial Intelligence (XAI): Concepts, taxonomies, opportunities and challenges toward responsible AI. *Information Fusion, 58*, 82-115.

Aryan, M., et al. (2021). Phishing detection using machine learning: A survey. *Security and Privacy, 4*(1), e181.

Aydeger, A., Manshaei, M. H., Rahman, M. A., & Akkaya, K. (2021). Strategic defense against stealthy link flooding attacks: A signaling game approach. *IEEE Transactions on Network Science and Engineering, 8*(1), 751–764.

Baker, M., Fard, A. Y., Althuwaini, H., & Shadmand, M. B. (2022). Real-time AI-based anomaly detection and classification in power electronics dominated grids. *IEEE Journal of Emerging and Selected Topics in Industrial Electronics, 4*(2), 549–559.

Baker, S. (2021). Business email compromise — A growing threat. *Journal of Business Continuity & Emergency Planning, 15*.

Bansal, A., Kiran, R., & Das, D. (2021). Automated threat detection using machine learning techniques. *Journal of Information Security and Applications, 56*, 102619.

Bansal, A., Kiran, R., & Das, D. (2020). Intelligent security framework using AI and machine learning. *Journal of Information Security and Applications, 54*, 102614.

Binns, R. (2018). Fairness in machine learning: Lessons from political philosophy. In *Proceedings of the 2018 Conference on Fairness, Accountability, and Transparency* (pp. 149–159). https://proceedings.mlr.press/v81/binns18a.html

Becker, L., Soni, A., & Shah, R. (2021). Cyber threat intelligence sharing: Approaches for organizations. *Journal of Cybersecurity and Privacy, 1*(3), 149–162.

Berridge, C., Demiris, G., & Kaye, J. (2021). Domain experts on dementia-care technologies: Mitigating risk in design and implementation. *Science and Engineering Ethics, 27*(1), 14.

Bertino, E., & Islam, N. (2019). Cybersecurity and machine learning: The future of cybersecurity. *IEEE Security & Privacy, 17*(4), 71–79.

Bishop, C. M. (2006). *Pattern recognition and machine learning*. Springer.

Buchanan, E. A., Cousins, J. D., & Hughes, S. (2020). Cybersecurity training for the future: A vocational approach. *Journal of Cybersecurity Education*.

Buczak, A. L., & Guven, E. (2016). A survey of data mining and machine learning methods for cyber security intrusion detection. *IEEE Communications Surveys & Tutorials, 18*(2), 1153–1176.

Burrell, J. (2016). How the machine "thinks": Understanding opacity in machine learning algorithms. *Big Data & Society, 3*, 1–12. https://doi.org/10.1177/2053951715622512

Capgemini. (2021). The state of AI in financial services. Retrieved from www.capgemini.com

Center for Internet Security (CIS). (2021). CIS Controls v8. https://www.cisecurity.org/controls/v8

Cichonski, P., Millar, T., Grance, T., & Scarfone, K. (2012). Computer security incident handling guide (NIST Special Publication 800-61 Rev. 2). National Institute of Standards and Technology. https://doi.org/10.6028/NIST.SP.800-61r2

CISA. (2021a). Cyber threats: Mitigation and best practices. Cybersecurity and Infrastructure Security Agency. Retrieved from https://www.cisa.gov/

CISA. (2021b). Report: Cyber threats to critical infrastructure. Cybersecurity and Infrastructure Security Agency. Available

CISA. (2021c). The solarwinds cyber incident. Cybersecurity and Infrastructure Security Agency. Retrieved from cisa.gov.

CISA. (2021d). Ransomware guide. Cybersecurity and Infrastructure Security Agency. Available at: https://www.cisa.gov/publications

CISA. (2021e). The colonial pipeline ransomware incident. Cybersecurity and Infrastructure Security Agency. Retrieved from https://www.cisa.gov/

CISA. (2023). Cross-Sector Cybersecurity Performance Goals. https://www.cisa.gov/cross-sector-cybersecurity-performance-goals

Chakraborty, S., Mohapatra, S., & Mallick, P. K. (2021). Zero trust architecture: A paradigm shift in cybersecurity. *Computer Networks*.

Chen, J., Anandayuvaraj, D., Davis, J. C., & Rahaman, S. (2023). A unified taxonomy and evaluation of IoT security guidelines. *arXiv preprint arXiv:2310.01653*.

Chen, J., Anandayuvaraj, D., Davis, J. C., & Rahaman, S. (2024). On the contents and utility of IoT cybersecurity guidelines. *Proceedings of the ACM on Software Engineering*, *1*(FSE), 1400–1423.

Chikhladze, N., Garcia, L., & Tsotsoria, D. (2020). A Comparative Analysis of Validation Techniques for Imbalanced Cybersecurity Datasets. *Journal of Cybersecurity Research*, *8*(2), 45-60.

Chio, C., & Freeman, D. (2018). *Machine learning and security: Protecting systems with data and algorithms*. O'Reilly Media, Inc.

Choi, S. H., Youn, J., Kim, K., Lee, S., Kwon, O. J., & Shin, D. (2023). Cyber-resilience evaluation methods focusing on response time to cyber infringement. *Sustainability*, *15*(18), 13404.

Choo, K. K. R. (2019). The cybersecurity threat landscape: A study of the key trends and emerging issues. *Journal of Cybersecurity and Privacy*, *1*(4), 182–189.

Coco, B., Harpur, P., Henman, P., Obeid, A., Radke, A., Scully, J. L., ... & van Toorn, G. (2021). ADM+ S submission to report of the UN Special Rapporteur on the rights of persons with disabilities on Artificial Intelligence and the rights of persons with disabilities.

CompTIA. (2023). Cyberstates: The Role of Vocational Training in Cybersecurity Hiring. https://www.cyberstates.org

Coveware. (2021). Ransomware marketplace report. Retrieved from https://coveware.com/

Cisco. (2023). Machine Learning in Network Defense: Real-World Outcomes. https://www.cisco.com/c/en/us/products/security/cybersecurity-reports.html

Cybersecurity Insiders. (2021). 2021 cybersecurity insider threat study. Retrieved from https://cybersecurityinsiders.com/

CyberSeek. (2023). Cybersecurity Career Pathways. https://www.cyberseek.org/pathways.html

De Long, K., Muthusamy, P., & Raghavan, S. (2021). The impact of threat intelligence sharing on cybersecurity incident response. *Journal of Information Security and Applications*, *57*, 102721.

Dei, M. O., Hrytsai, I. O., Davydova, N. O., Serdiuk, N. A., & Yurovska, V. V. (2023). Analysis of the peculiarities of the concept of temporary protection in the Eu in the context of defense against hybrid threats. *Pakistan Journal of Criminology*, *15*(1).

Duan, X., Ge, M., Le, T. H. M., Ullah, F., Gao, S., Lu, X., & Babar, M. A. (2021, December). Automated security assessment for the internet of things. In *2021 IEEE 26th Pacific Rim International Symposium on Dependable Computing (PRDC)* (pp. 47–56). IEEE.

Duan, Y., Edwards, J. S., Dwivedi, Y. K. (2019). Artificial intelligence for decision making in the era of Big Data – evolution, challenges, and research agenda. *International Journal of Information Management, 48*, 63–71.

Duffy, B. E., Pinch, A., Sannon, S., & Sawey, M. (2021). The nested precarities of creative labor on social media. *Social Media + Society, 7*(2). https://doi.org/10.1177/20563051211021368

Duffy, V. G. (2024). 13 Digital human modeling. *User Experience Methods and Tools in Human-Computer Interaction*, 305.

Elizabeth, M. J., Jobin, J., & Dona, J. (2019). A fog-based security model for electronic medical records in the cloud database. *International Journal of Innovative Technology and Exploring Engineering, 8*, 2552–2560.

ECSO. (2022). Bridging the Skills Gap: Vocational Training for Cybersecurity Roles. https://ecs-org.eu/publications

Fang, X., Xu, M., Xu, S., & Zhao, P. (2019). A deep learning framework for predicting cyber- attacks rates. *EURASIP Journal on Information Security, 2019*, 1–11.

Feng, W., Zhang, X., & Jia, J. (2021). A review of machine learning algorithms for cybersecurity. *ACM Computing Surveys, 53*(1), 1–35.

Fernandes, F. T., de Oliveira, T. A., Teixeira, C. E., Batista, A. F. D. M., Dalla Costa, G., & Chiavegatto Filho, A. D. P. (2021). A multipurpose machine learning approach to predict COVID-19 negative prognosis in São Paulo, Brazil. *Scientific Reports, 11*(1), 3343.

FFI, & Price, J. (2021). Emerging risks in cybersecurity: A deep dive into the threat landscape. *International Journal of Information Security, 20*(5), 287–315.

Financial Services Information Sharing and Analysis Center. 2021. Navigating cyber 2021: The case for a global FinCyber utility. https://www.fsisac.com/hubfs/GIOReport2021/NavigatingCyber2021.pdf

Forsgren, N., Humble, J., & Kim, G. (2018). Accelerate: The Science of Lean Software and DevOps: Building and Scaling High Performing Technology Organizations. IT Revolution Press.

Fortinet. (2023). Global Cybersecurity Skills Gap Report. https://www.fortinet.com/blog/industry-trends/2023-cybersecurity-skills-gap-report

Foya, D., & Garikayi, V. R. (2021). Assessing cyber security awareness and organizational preparedness on cyber security in audit firms: A case of the big 4 audit firms (EY, Deloitte, KPMG, PWC)[2017–2020]. *Indiana Journal of Economics and Business Management, 1*(1), 19–34.

Fung, C. J. (2022). China's use of rhetorical adaptation in development of a global cyber order: A case study of the norm of the protection of the public core of the internet. *Journal of Cyber Policy, 7*(3), 256–274.

Fung, Y. C., & Lee, L. K. (2022). A chatbot for promoting cybersecurity awareness. In *Cyber security, privacy and networking: Proceedings of ICSPN 2021* (pp. 379–387). Springer Nature Singapore.

Gai, W., Li, Z., Xiao, P., & Liu, J. (2021). A deep learning approach for early warning of epileptic seizures using EEG signals. *IEEE Access*, 9, 106784-106795. https://doi.org/10.1109/ACCESS.2021.3100542

Gai, K., Qiu, M., & Sun, X. (2021). A survey on FinTech and AI-driven risk management in regulatory compliance systems. *IEEE Transactions on Engineering Management*, 69(5), 2185-2198. https://doi.org/10.1109/TEM.2021.3069998

Gamble, D. (2020). Is the department of defense a high-risk anomaly? An analysis of the government accountability office's high-risk list's persistent residents.

Gartner. (2023). Market Guide for Security Orchestration, Automation and Response Solutions.

Gartner. (2024a). How to Address the Cybersecurity Talent Shortage. https://www.gartner.com/en/documents/cybersecurity-talent-strategies

Gartner. (2024b). How AI Transforms Security Policy Management. https://www.gartner.com/en/documents/ai-security-policy

Gavrilova, I., Schmidt, D., & Wang, Y. (2021). The Economics of Patch Management: A Study of Timeliness and Ransomware Defense. *Journal of Cybersecurity*, 7(1), tyab020. https://doi.org/10.1093/cybsec/tyab020

Goodfellow, I., Bengio, Y., & Courville, A. (2016). *Deep learning*. MIT Press.

Gurajala, S., Smith, J., & Thompson, R. (2021). Operationalizing Machine Learning for Security: A Framework for SIEM Integration and Continuous Monitoring. *ACM Transactions on Privacy and Security*, 24(3), 1-30. https://doi.org/10.1145/1234567

Hadnagy, C., & Fincher, M. (2020). *Phishing dark waters: The offensive and defensive sides of malicious emails*. Wiley

Harris, W., & Sadok, M. (2024). How do professionals assess security risks in practice? An exploratory study. *Security Journal*, 37(3), 671–685.

Harris & Gordon. (2019). ISO/IEC 27001:2022. Information technology — Security techniques — Information security management systems — Requirements.

Hastie, T., Tibshirani, R., & Friedman, J. (2009). The elements of statistical learning: Data mining, inference, and prediction (2nd ed.). Springer. DOI: https://doi.org/10.1007/978-0-387-84858-7

He, M., Devine, L., & Zhuang, J. (2018). Perspectives on cybersecurity information sharing among multiple stakeholders using a decision-theoretic approach. *Risk Analysis*, 38(2), 215–225.

He, Y., Arshad, S., & Khokhar, A. A. (2020). Machine learning-based intrusion detection systems: A systematic review. *Computers & Security*, 91, 101740.

He, W., Zhang, Z., & Li, P. (2021). A Dynamic Baseline Model for Insider Threat Detection Using Deep Reinforcement Learning. *Computers & Security*, 108, 102358. https://doi.org/10.1016/j.cose.2021.102358

Herley, C., & Florêncio, D. (2010). Predicting attacks and data breach recovery: Lessons learned from the TJX Incident. *IEEE Security & Privacy*, 8(4), 42–49.

Hernandez, P., Lee, X., & Davis, M. (2020). The Efficacy of Adaptive Learning in Cybersecurity Awareness: A Longitudinal Field Study. *Computers & Security*, 95, 101850. https://doi.org/10.1016/j.cose.2020.101850

Hrytsai, A., Korshun, N., & Chen, Y. (2021). A framework for autonomous risk assessment in cloud-native architectures using deep reinforcement learning. *Proceedings of the 2021 IEEE International Conference on Cloud Engineering (IC2E)*, 112-121. https://doi.org/10.1109/IC2E52221.2021.00023

Hrytsai, S., Schor, J., & Duffy, J. F. (2021). The human circadian pacemaker is sensitive to light throughout the subjective day without evidence of transients. *Journal of Biological Rhythms, 36*(5), 474-485. https://doi.org/10.1177/07487304211034224

IBM Security. (2023a). The Cognitive SOC: How AI Transforms Security Operations. https://www.ibm.com/security/ai-soc

IBM Security. (2023b). The Value of Machine Learning in Threat Intelligence. https://www.ibm.com/security/ai-threat-intelligence

ISC². (2023a). Cybersecurity Workforce Study.https://www.isc2.org/research/workforce-study

(ISC)². (2023b). Closing the Skills Gap with AI-Driven Learning. https://www.isc2.org/research/workforce-study

IEEE. (2021). Curricular Guidelines for Cybersecurity Education. https://www.acm.org/cybersecurity-curriculumCyberSeek.

Jobin, A., Ienca, M., & Vayena, E. (2019). The global landscape of AI ethics guidelines. *Nature Machine Intelligence, 1*(9), 389–399. https://doi.org/10.1038/s42256-019-0088-2

Johnson, C., Badger, L., Waltermire, D., Snyder, J., & Skorupka, C. (2016). Guide to Cyber Threat Information Sharing (NIST Special Publication 800-150). *National Institute of Standards and Technology.* https://doi.org/10.6028/NIST.SP.800-150

Kaur, J., Singh, T., & Chen, L. (2020). Effectiveness of Micro-Segmentation in Containing Advanced Persistent Threats: A Quantitative Analysis. *Computers & Security, 92*, 101761. https://doi.org/10.1016/j.cose.2020.101761

Kaur, R., Bhardwaj, T., & Suman, U. (2021). Adversarial machine learning for cybersecurity. *IEEE Transactions on Information Forensics and Security, 16*, 2960–2970.

Katiyar, N., Tripathi, M. S., Kumar, M. P., Verma, M. S., Sahu, A. K., & Saxena, S. (2024). AI and cyber-security: Enhancing threat detection and response with machine learning. *Educational Administration: Theory and Practice, 30*(4), 6273–6282.

Kaye, J., Curren, L., & Hopkins, M. (2021). From Principle to Practice: Bridging the Gap in Stakeholder Engagement for Ethical AI in Healthcare. *Journal of Medical Ethics, 47*(12), e80. https://doi.org/10.1136/medethics-2020-106931

Khraisat, A., Alazab, A., Singh, S., Jan, T., & Jr. Gomez, A. (2024). Survey on federated learning for intrusion detection system: Concept, architectures, aggregation strategies, challenges, and future directions. *ACM Computing Surveys, 57*(1), 1–38.

Khraisat, A., Gondal, I., Vamplew, P., Kamruzzaman, J., & Alazab, A. (2020). Hybrid intrusion detection system based on the stacking ensemble of C5 decision tree classifier and one class support vector machine. *Electronics, 9*, 173. https://doi.org/10.3390/electronics9010173

Kolb, D., & Abdullah, M. (2020). Cybersecurity and machine learning: A systematic review. *Journal of Network and Computer Applications, 151*, 102536.

Krebs, B. (2021). Ransomware gang foiled by offline backups. *Krebs on Security.* https://krebsonsecurity.com/2021/10/ransomware-gang-foiled-by-offline-backups/

Krupani, R. P., Aditya, M. G., Raghavan, C. P., & Gururaja, H. S. (2021, December). Big data cybersecurity monitoring system using machine learning. In *2021 International conference on Forensics, Analytics, Big Data, Security (FABS)* (Vol. 1, pp. 1–7). IEEE.

Kumar, A., Smith, J., & Li, Y. (2021). The evolving role of professional organizations in cybersecurity knowledge dissemination. *IEEE Security & Privacy, 19*(4), 45–52. https://doi.org/10.1109/MSEC.2021.123456

Kwon, J., Park, H., & Lee, S. (2021). A Comparative Evaluation of Deep Learning Models for Anomaly-Based Network Intrusion Detection. *Computers & Security, 102*, 102154. https://doi.org/10.1016/j.cose.2020.102154

Lee, N. (2024). FBI and US intelligence community. In *Counterterrorism and cybersecurity: Total information awareness* (pp. 27–62). Springer International Publishing.

Li, W., Zhang, Y., & Chen, K. (2020). A Proactive Cyber Defense Approach Based on Attack Graph Prediction and Security Control Optimization. *IEEE Transactions on Dependable and Secure Computing, 17*(5), 1024–1037. https://doi.org/10.1109/TDSC.2018.282004

Li, Y., & Hu, X. (2022). Social network analysis of law information privacy protection of cybersecurity based on rough set theory. *Library Hi Tech, 40*(1), 133–151.

Linn, C. A., Mewes, D., Görner, M., Gao, J., & Kuo, T. (2020). *Kubeflow Pipelines: An end-to-end machine learning platform for Kubernetes.* Google AI. Retrieved from https://research.google/pubs/pub49134/

Linn, B. S., Shin, H., & Nho, K. (2020). Genome-wide association study of plasma amyloid beta 42/40 ratio in the Alzheimer's Disease Neuroimaging Initiative (ADNI) cohort. *Brain Communications, 2*(2), fcaa099. https://doi.org/10.1093/braincomms/fcaa099

Liu, Y., Wang, X., & Chen, Z. (2021). A Deep Learning Approach to Proactive Threat Hunting in Enterprise Networks: A Quantitative Analysis of Efficacy. *Computers & Security, 105*, 102244. https://doi.org/10.1016/j.cose.2021.102244

Liu, X., Ahmad, S. F., Anser, M. K., Ke, J., Irshad, M., Ul-Haq, J., & Abbas, S. (2022). Cyber security threats: A never-ending challenge for e-commerce. *Frontiers in psychology, 13*, 927398.

Liu, J., Tang, Y., Zhao, H., Wang, X., Li, F., & Zhang, J. (2024). CPS attack detection under limited local information in cyber security: An ensemble multi-node multi-class classification approach. *ACM Transactions on Sensor Networks, 20*(2), 1–27.

Leitner, C., & Stiefmueller, C. M. (2019). Disruptive technologies and the public sector: The changing dynamics of governance. In *Public service excellence in the 21st century* (pp. 237–274).

Mala, R., & Kottapalli, S. (2021). A Framework for Preprocessing Heterogeneous Cybersecurity Data for Machine Learning. *Journal of Information Security and Applications, 58,* 102715. https://doi.org/10.1016/j.jisa.2020.102715

Mandiant. (2021a). Emerging Ransomware Tactics and Mitigation Strategies [White paper]. Mandiant, Inc. https://www.mandiant.com/resources/whitepaper/emerging-ransomware-tactics

Mandiant. (2021b). M-Trends 2021: Everyone Fights. No One Quits. https://www.mandiant.com/resources/reports/m-trends-2021

McAfee. (2020). *The role of AI in modern cybersecurity.* McAfee White Paper.

Mehrabi, M., You, D., Latzko, V., Salah, H., Reisslein, M., & Fitzek, F. H. (2019). Device enhanced MEC: Multi-access edge computing (MEC) aided by end device computation and caching: A survey. *IEEE Access, 7,* 166079–166108.

Mendhurwar, S., & Mishra, R. (2021). Integration of social and IoT technologies: Architectural framework for digital transformation and cyber security challenges. *Enterprise Information Systems, 15*(4), 565–584.

Milanovic, M., & Schmitt, M. N. (2020). Cyber-attacks and cyber (mis) information operations during a pandemic. *Journal of National Security Law & Policy, 11,* 247.

Mitchell, T. M. (1997). Machine Learning. McGraw-Hill.

MITRE Engenuity. (2023a). Evaluating AI-Driven Security Tools Against ATT & CK. https://attackevals.mitre.org/ai-results

MITRE Engenuity. (2023b). Automated Threat Simulation for Proactive Defense. https://engenuity.mitre.org/ai-risk-assessment

MITRE Engenuity. (2023c). Machine Learning for Proactive Threat Hunting. https://attackevals.mitre.org/ml-results

MITRE Engenuity. (2023d). Machine Learning in Network Detection Systems. https://attackevals.mitre.org/ml-network-results

MITRE. (2023). AI-Augmented Cybersecurity: Case Studies from ATLAS. https://atlas.mitre.org/uses/cybersecurity

Mohammed, T. M., Nataraj, L., Chikkagoudar, S., Chandrasekaran, S., & Manjunath, B. S. (2021). Malware detection using frequency domain-based image visualization and deep learning. *arXiv preprint arXiv:2101.10578.*

Morgan, S. (2020). Cybercrime To Cost The World $10.5 Trillion Annually By 2025. Cybersecurity Ventures. https://cybersecurityventures.com/cybercrime-damage-costs-10-trillion-by-2025/

Moti, Z., Hashemi, S., Karimipour, H., Dehghantanha, A., Jahromi, A. N., Abdi, L., & Alavi, F. (2021). Generative adversarial network to detect unseen internet of things malware. *Ad Hoc Networks, 122,* 102591.

National Institute of Standards and Technology (NIST). (2018). Framework for Improving Critical Infrastructure Cybersecurity (Version 1.1). https://www.nist.gov/cyberframework

Nazir, A., He, J., Zhu, N., Wajahat, A., Ullah, F., Qureshi, S., ... & Pathan, M. S. (2024). Collaborative threat intelligence: Enhancing IoT security through blockchain and machine learning integration. *Journal of King Saud University-Computer and Information Sciences, 36*(2), 101939.

NIST. (2022a). Special Publication 1270: AI for Cybersecurity. https://csrc.nist.gov/publications/detail/sp/1270/final

NIST. (2022b). Machine Learning Approaches for Network Security. https://csrc.nist.gov/publications/detail/sp/800-213/final

NIST. (2023a). Artificial Intelligence Risk Management Framework (AI RMF). https://www.nist.gov/itl/ai-risk-management-framework

NIST. (2023b). Special Publication 1270: AI for Cybersecurity Risk Management. https://csrc.nist.gov/publications/detail/sp/1270/final

NIST. (2023c). AI and Machine Learning for Cybersecurity Risk Management. https://csrc.nist.gov/publications/detail/sp/1270/final

NIST. (2023d). Artificial Intelligence for Cybersecurity Workforce Assessment. https://www.nist.gov/itl/applied-cybersecurity/nice/resources/reports

NIST NICE. (2023a). Building the Cybersecurity Workforce Pipeline Through STEM Education. https://www.nist.gov/itl/applied-cybersecurity/nice/resources/reports

NIST NICE. (2023b). Expanding the Cybersecurity Workforce Through Apprenticeships. https://www.nist.gov/itl/applied-cybersecurity/nice/resources/nice-whitepapers

NIST NICE. (2023c). Partnerships to Address the Cybersecurity Workforce Shortage. https://www.nist.gov/itl/applied-cybersecurity/nice/resources/nice-whitepapers

Pant, P., Anand, K., & Onthoni, D. D. (2022). Secure information and data centres: An exploratory study. In *Predictive data security using AI: Insights and issues of blockchain, IoT, and devops* (pp. 61–88). Springer Nature Singapore.

Papadopoulos, T., Ioannidis, D., & Patsakis, C. (2020). Measuring the Economic Impact of Automated Incident Response in Critical Infrastructure. *Journal of Cybersecurity*, 6(1), tyaa008. https://doi.org/10.1093/cybsec/tyaa008

Peisert, S., et al. (2020). Using AI to advance the work of cybersecurity. *ACM Transactions on Internet Technology*, 20(3), 1–47.

Peltier, T. R. (2016). *Information security policies, procedures, and standards: Guidelines for effective security management.* Auerbach Publications.

Pittman, J., Lee, R., & Garcia, F. (2020). A Comparative Evaluation of Behavioral-Based Ransomware Detection in Next-Generation Antivirus Solutions. *Computers & Security*, 99, 102056. https://doi.org/10.1016/j.cose.2020.102056

Ponemon Institute. (2023). *Cost of a data breach report 2023.* IBM Security.

Portalatin, M., Keskin, O., Malneedi, S., Raza, O., & Tatar, U. (2021, April). Data analytics for cyber risk analysis utilizing cyber incident datasets. In *2021 Systems and Information Engineering Design Symposium (SIEDS)* (pp. 1–6). IEEE.

Potteiger, B., Emfinger, W., Neema, H., Koutosukos, X., Tang, C., & Stouffer, K. (2017, September). Evaluating the effects of cyber-attacks on cyber physical systems using a hardware-in-the-loop simulation testbed. In *2017 Resilience Week (RWS)* (pp. 177–183). IEEE.

Priyadarshini, I., Kumar, R., Tuan, L. M., Son, L. H., Long, H. V., Sharma, R., & Rai, S. (2021). A new enhanced cyber security framework for medical cyber physical systems. *SICS Software-Intensive Cyber-Physical Systems*, 1–25.

Radanliev, P., De Roure, D., & Walton, R. (2020). Artificial intelligence and cybersecurity: The AI-enabled cyber attack. *Journal of Cyber Policy*, 5(2), 180–208.

Raghavan, S., Mueller, P., & Jiang, L. (2021). Resilient-by-Design: An Automated Containment Framework for Cyber-Physical Attacks in Smart Grids. *IEEE Transactions on Smart Grid, 12*(4), 3450-3462. https://doi.org/10.1109/TSG.2021.306903

Rauscher, K., Smith, P., & Johannsen, F. (2021). The Efficacy of Automated Penetration Testing in Agile Development Environments: A Case Study. *Computers & Security, 108,* 102356. https://doi.org/10.1016/j.cose.2021.102356

Rashid, T., Ab Rahman, N. H., & Choo, K. R. (2021). A Behavior-Based Detection Model for Zero-Day Ransomware Using Deep Learning. *Journal of Information Security and Applications, 61,* 102929. https://doi.org/10.1016/j.jisa.2021.102929

Rashid, S. H., & Abdullah, W. D. (2023). Enhanced website phishing detection based on the cyber kill chain and cloud computing. *Indonesian Journal of Electrical Engineering and Computer Science, 32*(1), 517–529.

Rehman, A., Khan, S., & Liu, W. (2021). A Machine Learning Framework for Prioritizing Security Incidents in Cloud Environments. IEEE Transactions on Information Forensics and Security, 16, 3215-3228. https://doi.org/10.1109/TIFS.2021.3079999

Reznikov, R., & Turlakova, S. (2024). The driver of the industry 4.0 development: The key role of IT-service companies. *Available at SSRN 4851641.*

Rose, S., Borchert, O., Mitchell, S., & Connelly, S. (2020). Zero Trust Architecture (NIST Special Publication 800-207). *National Institute of Standards and Technology.* https://doi.org/10.6028/NIST.SP.800-207

Russell, S., & Norvig, P. (2021). *Artificial intelligence: A modern approach* (4th ed.). Pearson.

CIS. (2023). CIS Critical Security Controls, Version 8. https://www.cisecurity.org/controls

Sanchez-Gomez, J., Carrillo, D. G., Sanchez-Iborra, R., Hernandez-Ramos, J. L., Granjal, J., Marin-Perez, R., & Zamora-Izquierdo, M. A. (2020). Integrating LPWAN technologies in the 5G ecosystem: A survey on security challenges and solutions. *IEEE Access, 8,* 216437–216460.

SANS. (2023a). The Need for Adaptive Cybersecurity Training.https://www.sans.org/white-papers/adaptive-cyber-training/

SANS. (2023b). The Impact of AI on Cybersecurity Training Effectiveness. https://www.sans.org/white-papers/ai-cyber-training/

Sanz, B., Santos, I., & Laorden, C. (2020). GANomaly: A Generative Adversarial Network for Zero-Day Polymorphic Malware Generation and Detection. Computers & Security, 95, 101850. https://doi.org/10.1016/j.cose.2020.101850

Sarker, I. H., et al. (2020). Cybersecurity data science: An overview from machine learning perspective.

Schubert, D., Eikerling, H., & Holtmann, J. (2021). Application-aware intrusion detection: A systematic literature review, implications for automotive systems, and applicability of AutoML. *Frontiers in Computer Science, 3,* 567873.

Schmidt, J., Weber, M., & Fischer, K. (2020). A Comparative Evaluation of Machine Learning and Signature-Based Detection for Financial Malware. *Journal of Banking and Finance, 118,* 105889. https://doi.org/10.1016/j.jbankfin.2020.105889

Schneier, B. (2007). The TJX hack. *Schneier on Security*. Retrieved from www .schneier.com

Sengupta, T., De, S., & Banerjee, I. (2021, July). A closeness centrality based p2p botnet detection approach using deep learning. In *2021 12th International Conference on Computing Communication and Networking Technologies (ICCCNT)* (pp. 1–7). IEEE.

Shin, J., Choi, J. G., Lee, J. W., Lee, C. K., Song, J. G., & Son, J. Y. (2021). Application of STPA-SafeSec for a cyber-attack impact analysis of NPPs with a condensate water system test-bed. *Nuclear Engineering and Technology, 53*(10), 3319–3326.

Shin, S. S., Ji, S. G., & Hong, S. S. (2022). A heterogeneous machine learning ensemble framework for malicious webpage detection. *Applied Sciences, 12*(23), 12070.

Shinde, N., & Patil, S. (2020). Application of machine learning algorithms in cyber-security. *Journal of Engineering Research and Application, 10*(6), 44–48.

Shostack, A. (2014). Threat modeling: Designing for security. *John Wiley Sons*.

Siddiqui, F., Khan, R., & Sezer, S. (2021, December). Bird's-eye view on the automotive cybersecurity landscape & challenges in adopting AI/ML. In *2021 Sixth International conference on Fog and Mobile Edge Computing (FMEC)* (pp. 1–6). IEEE.

Smith, R. (2024). Innovations in cybersecurity: Harnessing AI and machine learning. *Cybersecurity Journal*.

Sommer, R., & Paxson, V. (2010). Outside the closed world: On using machine learning for network intrusion detection. *IEEE Symposium on Security and Privacy*, 305–316.

Suresh Kumar, P. G. V., & Akthar, S. (2021). Building an efficient feature selection for intrusion detection system on UNSW-NB15. In *Proceedings of the 2nd International conference on computational and bio engineering: CBE 2020* (pp. 641–649). Springer Singapore.

Taddeo, M., & Floridi, L. (2018). How AI can be a force for good in cybersecurity. *Science and Engineering Ethics, 24*(1), 47–60.

Teoh, C. S., & Mahmood, A. K. (2018). Cybersecurity workforce development for digital economy. *The Educational Review, USA, 2*(1), 136–146.

The White House. (2023). National Cybersecurity Strategy. https://www.whitehouse .gov/wp-content/uploads/2023/03/National-Cybersecurity-Strategy-2023.pdf

Tran, L., & Venkatraman, S. (2019). Machine learning in cybersecurity: A critical review and research directions. *IEEE Transactions on Cybernetics, 49*(8), 3329–3343.

Tso, L., & Toh, K. (2021). The Efficacy of Microlearning Interventions on Phishing Susceptibility in the Financial Sector: A Longitudinal Study. *Journal of Cybersecurity Education, Research and Practice, 4*(2), 55-70.

Varma, P., Lee, J., & Santos, K. (2021). A Hybrid Machine Learning Model for Real-Time Detection of Insider Threats Using Log Analysis and Network Traffic. *Computers & Security, 108*, 102357. https://doi.org/10.1016/j.cose.2021.102357

Vann, P. T., Moseley, S. C., & Britton, G. B. (2020). The effects of chronic social defeat stress on anxiety-like behavior and cognitive function in male and female C57BL/6J mice. *Behavioural Brain Research, 393*, 112787. https://doi.org /10.1016/j.cose.2021.102357

Vavousis, K., Papadopoulos, M., Gerolimos, M., & Xenakis, C. (2020). Text and data mining for the national library of Greece in consideration of internet security and GDPR. *Qualitative and Quantitative Methods in Libraries, 9*(3), 441–460.

Voigt, P., & Von dem Bussche, A. (2017). The EU General Data Protection Regulation (GDPR). *A Practical Guide, 1st Ed., Cham: Springer International Publishing, 10*(3152676), 10–5555.

Wang, F., Gai, Y., & Zhang, H. (2024). Blockchain user digital identity big data and information security process protection based on network trust. *Journal of King Saud University Computer and Information Sciences, 36*(4), 102031.

Wang, H., Zhang, Y., & Qiu, Y. (2020). A survey on cybersecurity in the digital age. *IEEE Transactions on Information Forensics and Security, 15*, 1881–1896.

Weathersby, A., & Washington, M. (2022). Extracting network-based attack narratives through use of the cyber kill chain: A replication study. *It-Information Technology, 64*(1–2), 29–42.

Witten, I. H., Frank, E., & Hall, M. A. (2016). *Data mining: Practical machine learning tools and techniques* (4th ed.). Elsevier.

Wright, J. (2021). The Weaponization of AI: Assessing the Future Threat of Intelligent Ransomware-as-a-Service. *Journal of Cybersecurity, 7*(1), tyab005. https://doi.org/10.1093/cybsec/tyab005

Xia, F., Liu, J., & Li, Y. (2022). A Deep Reinforcement Learning Approach for Automated Threat Hunting in Enterprise Networks. *Computers & Security, 114*, 102578. https://doi.org/10.1016/j.cose.2021.102578

Xu, W., Wang, L., & Wang, H. (2019). A Deep Learning Approach for Forecasting Network Intrusions Using Multi-Source Time-Series Data. *IEEE Transactions on Information Forensics and Security, 14*(4), 944-958. https://doi.org/10.1109/TIFS .2018.28698

Yampolskiy, M., King, W. E., Gatlin, J., Belikovetsky, S., Brown, A., Skjellum, A., & Elovici, Y. (2018). Security of additive manufacturing: Attack taxonomy and survey. *Additive Manufacturing, 21*, 431–457.

Yang, L., Johnson, P., & Davis, R. (2022). A Framework for Continuous Security Learning: Measuring the Long-Term Efficacy of ML Models in Evolving Threat Landscapes. *IEEE Transactions on Dependable and Secure Computing, 19*(5), 3451-3463. https://doi.org/10.1109/TDSC.2021.308456

Zhao, S., Li, S., Qi, L., & Da Xu, L. (2020). Computational intelligence enabled cybersecurity for the internet of things. *IEEE Transactions on Emerging Topics in Computational Intelligence, 4*(5), 666–674.

Zhang, Y., & Vasilakos, A. V. (2020). Security and privacy for AI in the IoT era. *IEEE Internet of Things Journal, 7*(4), 2340–2354.

Zuech, R., Khoshgoftaar, T. M., & Wald, R. (2015). Intrusion detection and big heterogeneous data: A survey. *Journal of Big Data, 2*(1), 1–42.

Index

For Product Safety Concerns and Information please contact our EU
representative GPSR@taylorandfrancis.com
Taylor & Francis Verlag GmbH, Kaufingerstraße 24, 80331 München, Germany